The Cross-Cultural Workers Spiritual Survival Guide

14 Survival Tips to Help You Thrive in Your Calling

By Don Mingo

Table of Contents

Introduction

I SUPPOSE THE TERM MISSIONARY is adequate, but in today's world, it's viewed rather pejoratively. Perhaps better words are 'worker' along with the phrase 'Sent Ones.'

In the *Cross-Cultural Worker's Spiritual Survival Guide,* these words describing a person's call to take God's message of sacrificial love revealed in Jesus Christ to people of another culture are used interchangeably.

Worker—*ergatēs*—is the expression Jesus used in Matthew 9:37-38. "He said to his disciples, 'The harvest is great, but the *workers* are few. So pray to the Lord who is in charge of the harvest; ask him to send more *workers* into his fields.'"

Missionaries are workers who labor in the harvest fields of this world to share a message of forgiveness and reconciliation through Jesus Christ. Mark 6:7; Luke 10:1

The term missionary is from the Latin, *mittere* and *missionem. Mittere* means "release, let go, send, or throw." *Missionem* indicates, "the act of sending, dispatching; a release, a setting at liberty."[1] Missionaries are Sent Ones.

God calls Sent Ones and sends them out to share the Good News; Jesus Christ. As a Sent One, life becomes an adventure that few muster the courage to contemplate. It's not the normal life of those back home, but an extra-normal excursion of faith. It is a journey filled with extraordinary meetings, high seas travel, and exploits beyond what others can only dream.

Most of all, the worker's highest contentment is becoming the hands and feet of Jesus, bringing hope offered in the Gospel.

There is none more fulfilling than staring into faith's horizon and taking the next step that faith demands. To live on faith's edge, trusting God for your next steps is a life like no other.

But beware. Out there in the swells of service lies significant dangers. Perils that few workers consider or prepare themselves for before departing from their shores of familiarity. The enemy plots extensively against them, and the lack of readiness dashes many a worker's good intentions.

In the crests of service exists great exhilaration, but that is also where the greatest danger lies. Those voyages that see Sent Ones from all around the world converge unto their focal places often prove traumatic too.

The price is exorbitant but worth it. For it bears eternal rewards for both workers and every person who receives the message of Jesus Christ, the hope of the world.

Helping you finish the journey set out before you is the aim of this book. It is my passion to equip you to pursue your calling. An equipping that I was ill prepared for upon meeting the enemy in the Gospel trenches of spiritual warfare for the first time.

Rocks and Lifelines

I offer 14 Spiritual Survival Tips to help enhance your journey and strengthen your soul. Each tip seeks encouragement, introspection, reflection and refitting.

At the end of many of the chapters are navigation markers to encourage further thought with open-ended coaching questions posed to challenge you. These are:

 Sail On

At the end of many chapters, I suggest a *Sail On* to extend thought for momentum and action. Often workspace is provided for short journaling and thoughts. Other times, an exercise relating to the chapter will challenge development of your thoughts and actions. Please consider spending ample time here. Many of the processes offered come from decades of missionary reflection.

 True North

In *True North,* I offer Scriptures pertinent to that chapter. Sometimes a meaningful quote will follow or a historical reference. Of the Bible verses listed, I've deliberately chosen some obscure passages of Scripture rather than passages and verses that familiarity might encourage the reader to glance over. These Scriptures will hopefully challenge you to ponder your path or next steps you intend to take.

Lighthouse

Light House represents the dangers of a cross-cultural Sent One's journey, and the necessity to keep your spiritual eyes—soul—focused upon a fixed point. That fixed point will help guide you on your journey towards its end.

This book comes from out of both joy and trauma. I hope it will help ensure duty to your calling, a willingness to pay the price it most certainly will exact, and the perseverance to finish well.

For in starting few finish, and only in finishing is the prize obtained. Let us hear the words, "Well done good and faithful servant."

Beneath the Waters

IN 1976, GORDON LIGHTFOOT'S HIT, *The Wreck of the Edmund Fitzgerald,* shot to number one on the Canadian Charts and hit number two on US Billboard Hot 100.[2] The pop song marked the greatest misfortune of the Great Lakes shipping industry in the United States.

The SS Edmund Fitzgerald—an American Great Lakes freighter—sank in a Lake Superior storm on November 10, 1975. When launched on June 7, 1958, she was the largest ship on North America's Great Lakes. She remains the largest vessel to sink there.[3]

I was a junior in high school in Minnesota the year the Fitzgerald sank in 535 feet of water off the shores of Lake Superior. It caught my attention as the news media highlighted the tragedy, and everyone—it seemed—talked about the ship's mysterious disappearing.

Captain Peter Pulcer skippered the Fitzgerald. Pulcer was known for piping music day and night over the ship's intercom while passing through Lakes Huron and Erie. He entertained spectators at the Soo Locks between Lakes Superior and Huron with a running commentary about the ship.[4] Her size, record-breaking performance, and the "DJ captain" endeared Edmund Fitzgerald to boat watchers.[5]

On the Fitzgerald's last day, the serving captain—Ernest McSorley—radioed his last words while caught in a midday hurricane force storm.

5

"We are holding our own."

With that, he vanished below the waters with 28 other crew members never to be heard from again.[6]

The wreck of the 729-foot "laker" was also a $24 million loss of an engineering marvel—a ship considered a Great Lakes workhorse as it racked up seasonal records for its cargo hauling abilities.[7]

This tragedy exposed the weaknesses and flaws of a vast industry. It led to changes in Great Lakes shipping regulations and practices that included mandatory survival suits, depth finders, positioning systems, increased freeboards, and more frequent inspections of vessels.[8]

The Edmund Fitzgerald now sits at the bottom of Lake Superior. That renown ship is a tale of what once was. No one knows what caused the vessel to sink. The only consensus is that the storm's winds and waves played a major role in the sinking. A tempest the Edmund Fitzgerald was ill-prepared to meet on that fateful afternoon.

The event resonates with me. Not so much because of its historical tragedy, but because of the similarities with missionaries observed over the years, including myself. The Fitzgerald tells of a crew caught unaware in waters they knew so well. *Holding their own,* they served to their end, slipping beneath the waters unaware of the defects that made them vulnerable to such a fate.

Missionaries often do the same. Finding themselves surrounded by stormy waters of life and ministry, they continue sending out their communiques, emails, social medias, and letters stating, "We are holding our own." All the while unaware that their ships—lives, relationships, and ministries—are taking on water. Their breached souls allow the waves to drag them into the depths and despair.

> *Does anyone know where the love of God goes*
> *When the waves turn the minutes to hours?*
> *The searches all say they'd have made Whitefish Bay*
> *If they'd put fifteen more miles behind her*
> *They might have split up or they might have capsized*

6

They may have broke deep and took water
And all that remains is the faces and the names
Of the wives and the sons and the daughters

5th Stanza of *The Wreck of the Edmund Fitzgerald*
by Gordon Lightfoot

Survival Tip #1

Accept Your New Normal

*We who have Christ's eternal life need to
throw away our own lives.*

George Verwer – Founder of Operation Mobilisation

NOUN—ADJECTIVE: *Normal,* something that is usual and ordinary; it is what people expect.[9]

Your new normal as a missionary is anything but normal. Not if you define normal as that which your friends and family require for life.

The Quest for Normal

After our first term on the field—six years—we returned 'home' to Minnesota in the United States. There was plenty of reacquainting with family, friends, and churches. During those first few months of furlough, an overwhelming sense of missing out on something crept up on me.

While slogging it out in Africa, friends and family gained cars, boats, houses—enormous houses—and surrounded themselves with all kinds of niceties. They talked about their 401k's retirement plans, timeshares, and cabins up North.

Their normal did not reflect my normal. *Normal* burrowed itself into my soul, setting off a year-long struggle. I remember thinking, "They are so much further ahead of us. We will never get anything as nice as that."

When invited over to a friend's home, an empty sense of loneliness awaited. Kathy—my lifelong friend and spouse—mentioned my unusual quietness during those visits. Quietness in a pit of emptiness that whispered, "I want their normal too."

A normal where you're not always the visitor. The only member of the family that doesn't make it to Christmas gatherings. The one who misses out on most family events.

A normal that doesn't make you feel like a foreigner in your own culture, your own church, or your own family for that matter. A normal that can answer the question, "So, where are you from?"

To me, home was a place where I could have the fun that was left undone. When I was lonely, and when I was blue, I thought of a place I called home. Except that home didn't exist anymore.

If only someone those many years ago helped me see that my normal as a Sent One was an exceptional new normal surpassing all the other normals of my friends and family back home.

The Missionary's New Normal

Normal is defined as "conforming to a standard; usual, typical, or expected." [10] As missionaries, we don't live a standard, usual, typical, or expected life.

Our new normal is a life of exceptional living. Rare occurrences. New cultures. The beauty of speaking other languages. Thinking in a language that adds a dimension of thought beyond the language you learned as a child.

Dreaming in those languages.

Singing in new tongues.

Experiencing foods you never tasted back home.

To see places most can only view on the internet.

There is constant travel. Navigating the world's airports. Then, there are the people!

Drinking a cup of *shay*—Palestinian Tea—with a man in his shop in Bethlehem, Israel.

Sitting with an old Zulu man under a Mkhamba tree in the mountains of Natal, South Africa, drinking an African beverage.

Meeting the Reindeer People of Mongolia.

Or, welcoming a Zulu King in South Africa learning to address him, "Wena wendlovu bayede inkosi." Your majesty, I salute you, oh King.

Learning a few words in Tupian to say to a Guarani man in Paraguay, "Ñandejára rohayhu ndeve." God loves you.

Unfortunately, a Sent One's new normal finds high exposure to human suffering in Third World cultures as well. Starving Africans. Cemeteries filled with black children whose only deficiency was their birthplace where medications so common in the First World are limited.

Normal is hard to find in densely populated megacities where smog blackens the lungs and reduces visibility. Or serving in a part of the world marked with conflict that exacts horrible trauma upon its people.

Normal—what people back home enjoy—is the challenge that often sinks many missionaries. That kind of normal doesn't exist. Not for me. Not for many missionaries I've spoken with over the years.

Here's the thing, that's ok! Normal need not be a condition we fear, if… you will surrender it for a new normal. A *missionary normal* that very few ever experience.

Your normal can provide an exciting adventure because outside of 'normal' exists a lifestyle and calling that makes the *missionary normal* a most incredible satisfying life.

Most of all, let your normal be seated in Jesus Christ.

Sail On

What does your new normal look like? How does it differ from your old normal? If not yet on the field, what do you anticipate your new normal to look like? How does your normal identify with Jesus Christ?

 True North

Now may the Lord of peace himself give you his peace at all times and in every situation.

2 Thessalonians 3:16

I have told you all this so that you may have peace in me. Here on earth you will have many trials and sorrows. But take heart, because I have overcome the world.

Jesus – John 16:33

 Light House

Jesus is our light house. Our enduring normal. In the changes that inevitably come in missionary life, Jesus is our anchor that secures us in waves of unavoidable change.

Most of all, remember to smile.

Survival Tip #2

Don't Idolize Your Expectations

Is it true... that in Jerusalem
I can erase my sins... Is it true?

Balian of Ibelin in *The Kingdom of Heaven*
— Orlando Bloom

A COURSE MAPPED OUT UPON expectations leads to disheartening destinations. Expectations see many workers resigning from the field shortly after their arrivals. Others, after years of service, return home believing their efforts wasted. Why? Because an expectation can never be fully met.

I've watched the movie *The Kingdom of Heaven* several times. The film is a highly inaccurate portrayal of historical events of that time.

Balian, played by Orlando Bloom, asked his wayward father, Godfrey de Ibelin, "Is it true... that in Jerusalem I can erase my sins... Is it true?" His father—Liam Neeson—answers, "We'll find out together."

They travel to a port city in Italy and set sail. Upon arriving in Jerusalem, it is anything else than what Balian imagined. His life is marked by struggle, opposition, and disenchantment. Balian's expectation of his New Jerusalem crashes in disbelief and doubt with the realities of what Jerusalem is, a place full of people struggling as much as the people back home in Italy.

Watching the movie for the first time with Kathy, I said, "That scene reminds me of missionaries." She wrinkled up her nose and said, "Really? How so?"

Just like Balian, who went to Jerusalem with a narrow view of the people and life, Jerusalem was based on his aspirations, not the realities of life there. So too, missionaries often enter their *mission fields* of service with high expectations based upon their own cultural mindsets. They lack familiarity with the country in which they intend to live, crafting their outlooks and beliefs towards a people they know little of or understand.

Expectations are the graveyard of missionaries. That somehow life on *the mission field*—a pejorative term—will fulfill me. That people previously unknown to me will somehow line up towards my fanciful desires and fill my assumption bucket full. Assumptions that require people and situations to act in a manner the missionary deems correct.

I hear it all the time. A missionary in despair, citing, "Things just didn't work out the way I thought they would."

Or, "Life on the field wasn't at all like those short-term missions trips I took."

And, "Those missionaries really changed from the first time I met them."

Still, "The people weren't anything like I thought they'd be."

There's something inherently short cited about expecting people of another culture to bow to your anticipations of them to satisfy your

14

expectations. *I'm expecting...* is a presumption you'll miss by a long shot almost every time.

It sort of resembles Disney's Jiminy Cricket singing to Pinocchio, *"When you wish upon a star makes no difference who you are. Anything your heart desires will come to you."*

> 'I'm expecting' is a presumption you'll miss by a long shot almost every time.

There's a tad bit of a problem with that wonderful little song. It's not true either. Not even close. Wish all you want upon your star, but unless you adjust your expectations, you'll run aground, dashing your hopes upon rocks of unfulfillment.

I'm hoping that... Once we received a group from Wisconsin at the airport in Johannesburg, South Africa. Leaving the airport for a 4-hour drive to Ladysmith, two people talked about their reasons for making the trip.

One woman said, "I'm hoping that God will do something special in my heart during our visit here in South Africa."

Ten days later, I asked, "Anything special happen in your heart these past ten days?" She responded, "I can't wait to get back home to get a good hamburger."

I smiled and grunted inside, "Well, that's special. Very special."

Another missionary spending only a year on the field shared, "I thought missionary life was more spiritual."

I asked, "What does 'spiritual' look like to you?" She responded, "I don't know, but... just not like this. I was hoping for so much more."

Last year, we joined a large group of missionaries on a retreat in Central America. Many conversations with those wonderful people revealed a need for spiritual renewal. There's something about missionary life that grinds the life out of you.

One missionary who enjoyed windsurfing spoke the most profound words of the week at that retreat. Speaking in our group, he said, "When there's no wind in my sail, no matter how hard I try, surfing will not happen. No matter my intentions, I'm not going anywhere."

He continued, "It doesn't do much good serving if we hang limp in a windless walk with God. If my walk with God doesn't power my actions and attitudes, I lose hope. We all do."

Fix Them Mentality. A fresh group of missionaries sat in Johannesburg, South Africa in a breakout session of a conference. The moderator of the group asked, "What do you want to accomplish here?"

Missionary after missionary shared their goals and aspirations. One missionary stood out, "I will share Jesus with these people. They need to receive Jesus and live like Christians."

The moderator—a black South African—was brilliant. He responded, "How do Christians live?" The young missionary shared a list of how every Christian ought to live.

Then the moderator smiled and reshaped his question, "Is that how Christians live in your church back home?"

"Well, yes, I suppose it is."

The moderated replied, "Ok, but is that how African Christians here in South Africa must live too?"

No one in the group answered.

He persisted, "What is it you can bring to this country—my country—and to these people—my people—that we truly need?"

The young missionary looked befuddled.

Again, no one answered. Then the African moderator grinned and said, "Good, this is a small step in the right direction."

A Touch from God. Another couple once shared, "We went to the field to get away from the busyness of life and get closer to God."

It baffles me a bit when missionaries expectations' speak of getting nearer to God on the field. Is God's closeness based upon topography, location, and setting? God's proximity isn't any more accessible in one place over another. James admonishes, "*Come close to God,* and *God will come close to you.* Wash

16

your hands, you sinners; purify your hearts, for your loyalty is divided between God and the world." James 4:8 Emphasis mine.

Before a cross-cultural worker leaves for the field, closeness to God is a virtue needing mastery first.

Begin an Adventure. For me, missionary life marked an exciting adventure. Moving to Africa! Learning the intricate clicks of the Zulu language. Helping Zulu Christians establish their churches. Helping care for sick children.

You know when the adventure ends? When you stop taking pictures of the country. When the newness wears off, and that new place becomes your home. Where adventure ends and daily living begins.

I learned that if it's only adventure you're seeking, then you'll chase your tail looking for one new high after another.

Turning Your Expectations into Expectancy

A missionary couple home on a furlough after years of service in Eurasia shared, "When they recruited us—referring to the American church they attended—they told us how fulfilling and rewarding missionary life would be."

The wife looked me in the eye and said, "It was a lie. Nothing worked out like they said it would. Nothing. I mean, sure, in the beginning, it excited us, the adventure that lay ahead of us. We would build a big church with a women's shelter, a place to feed hungry children, an institute to train leaders, and, well... but none of that worked out. Nothing prepared us for all the disappointments."

Expectation is "a belief that someone will or should achieve something."[11] It's a belief that something should or must happen in a particular way and sequence. Or that someone or something should possess a particular set of qualities or behaviors.[12]

Expectation probably results in more missionary casualties than any other single cause. Expectations are the graveyards of many Sent One's callings and dreams.

17

Unfortunately, this happens when the root of a missionary's expectation occurs from making good intentions the source of their fulfillment. Not the object of worship—Love God—and the aim of service; serve others.

I was there. When leaving for South Africa the first time, my aspirations and dreams flowed from the intent of, "This is what my missionary life must look like for me to be successful." As missionaries, we do this all the time.

> **Expectations probably results in more missionary casualties than any other single cause.**

- When I get to the field, my house must be like…
- This is what I will do when I…
- We will build a big…
- The missionary team I will serve on will be…
- Following God's leading in my life will…
- I'm raising enough money to purchase…

Then the bottom drops out when:
- It wasn't at all what I thought it would be like.
- I was so lonely.
- Nothing was the same as my short-term mission trips.
- My housing wasn't adequate.
- There was too much violence in the country.
- The veteran missionaries were impossible to work with.
- I wasn't sure what my responsibilities were.
- The veteran missionary was a workaholic and expected the same from me.
- My relationship with the missionaries who invited us to join them changed.
- I'm just a workhorse for the older missionaries.
- As soon as we arrived, the veteran missionary took a furlough, leaving us in charge of everything.
- The local people didn't appreciate me.

- Our home church forgot about us.
- My sending church got a new pastor.
- My home church suffered a split.
- My sending agency doesn't really care.
- The missionaries couldn't get along.
- God called us, but nothing was advancing the ministry there. We were going nowhere.
- I failed.
- It was boring. There was nothing to do.
- Financially we couldn't make it.
- The people over there were horrible. They lie, cheat, and steal.
- We didn't feel safe.
- My spouse didn't like the people or place.
- I didn't feel valued.
- Other missionaries ignored me.
- The team I was on was toxic.
- No one listened to me.
- It was like, "You're new here. In five or six years, maybe you'll have an opinion we'll want to listen to."
- It was way different from what I thought it would be. *Way different*!

Expectational Killers

Repeatedly, missionaries who've served on the field share, *"It wasn't anything like we expected."*

An entire missionary team came from the same wonderful church. Several years went into planning, fundraising, and team building. Before all the team members arrived on the field, their home church suffered a devastating split. This resulted in half the congregation leaving to start their own church. Before the last member arrived on the field, that missionary team split too.

Team members siding with the dissenting group leaving the church packed their bags and returned home. It overwhelmed the remaining team members. One young missionary stated, *"It wasn't supposed to be like this."*

A common statement repeatedly rehearsed by discouraged missionaries coming off the field is, *It was nothing like I thought it would be.*

"What was it supposed to be like?" The conversation continued for many hours over several days.

The dream of one complete, harmonious team of six couples from their home church to live and serve the beautiful people of an African country changed irrevocably. Fortunately, those who remained on the field enjoyed love and support from their church, pastors, and staff.

The Problem with Expectations

When expectations defines not so much what missionary life will look like, but what it *must* **look like**, then expectation turns from anticipation into an idol.

Yes, you know, one of those Old Testament handmade objects that people of antiquity created with their own hands in their own image and then bowed down and worshipped. In this, an expectation develops into an idol as thought demands *this is the way it must be for me.*

Check Your Expectations

Take a moment, please. Think about your expectations for your missionary work. Describe your expectations. Write them down.

Start with, "This is what I expect or expected my missionary life and ministry to look like once I arrive or arrived on the field." Now ask, "What or who is the object of that expectation? God? Others? Or… maybe—just maybe—ME?"

Expectation's Misguided Prayer

Dear God, when I get to the field, please give me the accommodations my heart desires. You know, that one with a front yard, in that neighborhood I like, with the gigantic picture windows.

Oh God, please make the other missionaries become subservient to my hopes for my missionary success.

God, you said in your Word, "We have not because we ask not." Therefore, I ask that you fulfill my expectations because Jesus said that if we have even a little faith, we can move mountains. I expect, therefore I am.

And you've placed deep in my heart a vision for the work. I know what's best for me and my ministry. So, make it so.

One more thing, God. Prepare the national people whom I will lead in your ways. You know, so they do what I know you want them to do through me.

Oh, and if it doesn't work out, I will be very disappointed.

Here I come!
Amen.

I love the words of Milton in *Paradise Regained*:

Much of the Soul they talk, but all awry;
And in themselves seek virtue; and to themselves
All glory arrogate, to God give none

21

I think—I know it was true for me—that missionary work often becomes too much about us—what we want—and not about *the Jesus we claim to preach and follow.*

Where do your expectations originate? Please think about this question. Where do notions of what your missionary experience should—*must*—look like arise?

Missionary expectations for life and service often develop from the deck of our own perspectives and desires. Before we've even left our shores for a distant land, we've often defined life and ministry before arriving—a definition that will surely change; most always must change.

Expectational Disappointments

As I pen these words, the coronavirus—COVID-19—has struck the world. The pandemic closed the borders of many countries. The missionary life and ministry we've known have probably changed forever.

For us—Kathy and I—rather than touching down in Nairobi, Kenya, as expected for a three-month tour of service with missionaries, I sit here before my computer in Granbury, Texas. My e*xpectation* of serving missionaries in Africa is no more. At least not this year.

It brings me back to my boating days again. Missionary life bears much in common with my water experiences of the past.

For example, I knew a bit about water after years of boating in Minnesota. None of that prepared me for the rough, turbulent waters of Sodwana Bay off the coast of South Africa. My expectation of sailing and water changed immensely the first morning we hit waves of the Indian Ocean that enveloped our small vessel that day.

As we heaved up and down in the trough of waves, our little 12-man boat disappeared as each wave crested. With every wave, our boat's visibility vanished from shore. Five minutes on the water that morning shattered my expectations of enjoyment. Seasickness slew me as I hung onto the side of the boat in an ill stupor, unable to take part in our dive.

Experience from piloting a 19ft bass boat on a 1500-acre lake in Northern Minnesota doesn't match sailing in a 60 ft catamaran out of Durban, South Africa into the Indian Ocean.

It's the same with missionary life and work. Little within a missionary's passport culture prepares expectations to reflect any reality of what we'll experience in a new culture.

And many times, this is exactly what we as missionaries do. Expectations often demand trying to impose your desires upon God, yourself, and, most likely, upon the people you're called to serve. Expectations demand that others become subservient to its will.[13]

> **Where do your expectations originate?**

My Zulu pastors in South Africa often spoke English based on their Zulu grammar. During our vision meetings they used to say, *"Let's not visionate what God is not visionating for us."* While the grammar is off, the truth of the statement is spot-on. Don't visionate that which God is not visionating for you.

When we build mission strategies around expectations, expectations become the fulcrum upon which we conduct our activities, not the Gospel. We think God should comply and conform to our way of thinking. It's a far cry from the apostle Paul's words, "Yes, I try to find common ground with everyone doing everything I can to save some." 1 Corinthians 9:22

What if our expectations defined heaven? And what if heaven turned out exactly the way we expected it to feel and look like?

Now contrast that with, "That is what the Scriptures mean when they say, 'No eye has seen, no ear has heard, and no mind has imagined what God has prepared for those who love him.'" 1 Corinthians 2:9

One of the most fascinating aspects about missionary life is that we don't have it all figured out. It requires living on the faith's edge, trusting God to meet our needs while guiding us in our God-ventures. Journeys and unfamiliar experiences add variety to an amazing, unique lifestyle that few ever experience.

But expectations can squelch faith big-time!

Expectancy Better Aids Us

Expectancy, though closely related to *expectations,* is a unique process of thinking. Expectancy is defined as an "anticipatory belief or desire."[14] Think of it as an anticipation without the unreasonably high demands of an expectation.

James, the half-brother of Jesus, dealt with this very issue. He wrote:

Look here, you who say, 'Today or tomorrow we are going to a certain town and will stay there a year. We will do business there and make a profit.' How do you know what your life will be like tomorrow? Your life is like the morning fog—it's here a little while, then it's gone. *What you ought to say is, "If the Lord wants us to, we will live and do this or that."*

James 4:13-15, Emphasis Mine

Expectancy anticipates the adventure without defining its destination. It discovers the journey rather than dictating it.

Expectancy Rests With God

A Scripture I've grown to cherish is Proverbs 3:5-6:

Trust in the Lord with all your heart;
  do not depend on your own understanding.
Seek his will in all you do,
  and *he will show you which path to take.*

24

What if—just what if—we leaned not so much upon our own desire of *this is what I expect it to look like*? What if we learned instead to pursue with expectancy God's leading in our missionary lives and endeavors?

Expectancy sourced in God finds a surer footing than expectations adrift in self-centered aspirations. Let your expectancy become God leading you into fresh adventures and discoveries.

 Sail On

Take a piece of paper, maybe from your journal. Or perhaps on your computer, create a new file—landscape portrait. Divide the page into two columns. On the top of one column, write *My Expectations*. Over to the next column, write *My Expectancies*.

When finished, compare the two columns. Where does faith come into your picture of missionary life? What about idolatry? What adjustments do you need to make to your expectations? How can you turn them into expectancies?

 True North

The hopes of the godly result in happiness, but the expectations of the wicked come to nothing.

Proverbs 10:28

My soul, wait silently for God alone, For my expectation is from Him.

Psalm 62:5 NKJV

According to my earnest expectation and hope that in nothing I shall be ashamed, but with all boldness, as always, so now also Christ will be magnified in my body, whether by life or by death.

Phil 1:20 NKJV

 Light House

Turn your expectations of what missions must look like into expectancies of what God can do through you to serve him and others.

Try smiling today.

Survival Tip #3

Don't Anchor Yourself In Today's Certainties

Hold everything in your hands lightly otherwise it
hurts when God pries your fingers open.

Corrie Ten Boom

IN 1994, JUST A FEW months before the first fully democratic elections in
South Africa, the country was in turmoil. In our ministry area of Northern Natal,
young men brandished AK 47's in the villages and townships. Political parties
previously outlawed under the white Apartheid government vied for political
emergence. The country was a tinderbox ready to ignite.

The United States Consulate in Durban informed us—and many other
Americans—of evacuation plans should the country erupt into a civil war. This
event marked our eighth year living in South Africa.

Having barely gained fluency in the Zulu language, planting our third church, and our sons beginning to enter high school in Ladysmith, the last thing I wanted to do was leave South Africa.

In my middle thirties, we'd just gotten started. Plans were in the making for some extraordinary attempts at ministry with the beginning of an Orphan Care Center in Mkhamba Gardens across the street from our home. But election conundrums produced angst and anxiety.

Would we be forced to leave the place we had just made home? Then the Holy Spirit delivered a wonderful Scripture to my heart.

We can make our plans, but the LORD determines our steps.

Proverbs 16:9

During this process, I wrote in my journal, "Live every day like you will stay forever, but may need to leave tomorrow. Live and enjoy life today, like you'll be where you are for the rest of your life. But don't cling excessively to your lifestyle, things, friends, and ministry. For if events wrench them from your life, it's painful." This mindset is just as true for me today as it was over thirty years ago when I wrote in these words in my journal.

> Live everyday like you will stay forever, but may need to leave tomorrow.

Anchored in Uncertainties

Here Today, Gone Tomorrow

As I write the pages of this book, several distraught missionaries communicated with me their disappointment of being ordered out of their

28

countries of ministry. Because of the Coronavirus, their mission agencies required them to return to their passport countries.

Now—after another four months—scores of missionaries departed from their fields of ministry, returning to their home countries seeking haven from COVID-19. Other workers holed themselves up in apartments and houses around the world under strict lockdowns.

One missionary couple, having arrived on the field only two months before Covid burst on the scene, sit in an apartment in a major city in Europe with their three small children. They've endured over 100 days of isolation and lockdown in a city they barely know.

For many, in a moment's notice, workers who'd spent decades living and serving in one place, uprooted themselves and returned "home." A home they found more foreign than the place they left. Questions of finances, plans, and longevity upended themselves in the new era of COVID-19, marking an epic challenge to missions.

Other missionaries shared stories of having to leave their homes, belongings, and friends because of newly enacted laws. Governments, visa revocations, sudden losses of financial support, health issues, trauma, and family emergencies changed lives irrevocably. I understand.

In 2006, we said goodbye to the town where we raised our sons. Selling most of our furniture and personal effects, we started all over again back *home* in a place that felt more foreign than the first day we entered South Africa.

Three years later, we settled into a brand new home built for us by some wonderful people in the church we pastored in Northern Minnesota. There I purposed to never move again. Ha!

Five years later we gave up our American dream in Northern Minnesota—a placed I loved—to enter missions again.

Perhaps the move was due partly to my dissatisfaction with pastoring an American church filled with petty first-world complaints.

Maybe it was *the always on the move syndrome* that plagues so many cross-cultural workers, who because of the ease of modern travel never seem able to settle down in any one place for long. Like Dorothy in The Wizard of Oz, they look somewhere over the rainbow for bluer skies.

We sensed God definitely leading us back into missions to help missionaries cope with the extraordinary pressures they face today. Pressures few non-missionaries can understand, regardless of how many trips they've taken to the foreign field.

As I sit here in front of my computer screen typing these words, we—Kathy and I—planned to be waking up and heading to the airport in Nairobi, Kenya to depart for Tanzania.

We planned on speaking at the S.A.L.T. Conference to over 100 missionaries in Arusha, Tanzania. After the conference ended, we intended to travel onto Ladysmith, South Africa. We looked forward to visiting the place we'd live and served at for over twenty years. Most of all, seeing our dearest friends.

A year's worth of planning went into the expected venture. For the first time in my life, health problems also became an issue. My heart focused itself upon *perhaps this is the last time visit to South Africa.* But… now…

Here we just sit on Lake Granbury in Texas. Like so many other missionaries, we made our plans, but COVID-19, which exploded onto the worldwide scene, changed all that.

Don't Hold on to Certain Uncertainties

Again, I'm reminded not to hold on to plans and anticipations so tightly as recent events ripped a year's worth of planning from my fingers. Yet… had we arrived at Jomo Kenyatta International Airport in Kenya as planned, we'd have found ourselves stranded as the governments of Tanzania and South Africa closed their airports.

A sense of uselessness overtook me for a brief time. Meetings were cancelled for the entire year. What to do? Where would the finances come from if our churches could not send financial support? Then, a better question surfaced, "How can I best serve now in these present circumstances?"

> Don't hold on to certain uncertainties.

Well... that's the sanitized version anyways. You know, the adaptation we share in our missionary reports, updates, and talks. My heart really screamed out, "NOW WHAT AM I SUPPOSED TO DO?"

You know what? God spoke. God always speaks. It's just often the case that we are rarely listening. His sweet Holy Spirit said to me,

Don, My Presence is here and now. Learn to see me, sense me, and feel me in your current situation rather than looking for Me in another place you're not at right now. Stop looking towards where you are not, and see Me right here, where you are.

An elderly missionary recently encouraged, "Unless you anchor yourself in God, you'll struggle with every aspect of missionary life." What do you attach yourself to, relying upon it or them, to steady you during tough times? Times which surely visit all missionaries.

Anchors

Growing up, every summer marked a highlight of boyhood. Anticipation began in May for "vacation" at Great-Grandpa and Grandma's lake.

Nestled on a channel connecting two lakes in Northern Minnesota stood a small, yellow, white-trimmed two-bedroom cabin. My great-grandparents built the little cabin in the 1940s. Great Grandpa died of a stroke in 1959, and it fell upon my grandfather, the only son, to manage the family property.

31

At that lake, "way up North," I learned how to fish for Walleye, Northern Pike, and a host of other creatures teaming under the waters just outside of the cabin's front porch.

Trolling was grandpa's favorite method of fishing. It involved dropping a lure to a certain depth into the water and dragging it behind the boat. The forward motion of the boat kept the artificial bait active, deceiving fish to strike the lure. Grandpa loved trolling, observing the wildlife and cabins on the rugged hills of the shoreline.

The Maryanne

The Maryanne—named after my great-grandma—was a 1950s 18ft wooden hull Chris Craft boat. Grandpa jettisoned the 75 horsepower, preferring a Mercury Hurricane Mark 25 outboard motor. Remember him saying, "With so many family members using this boat, that 75 horsepower would have gotten someone killed!"

Summer after summer grandpa drove that beautiful old wooden hall lady up and down the shorelines of Roosevelt Lake. Dragging our various spinners, lazy Ikes, and spoons from great grandpa's trolling rods marked a magic two weeks of life every summer.

Upon reaching thirteen, grandpa began giving boating lessons in his 14 ft. Alumacaft bare bones fishing boat. Grandma bought it for him one Christmas. It affectionately became known as grandpa's boat.

In that aluminum bottom boat with a 5-horse power Johnson motor, grandpa taught me the art of boating. From a thirteen-year-old's perspective, it felt as if I captained a ship through the Great Lakes.

In the many instructions and trainings grandpa offered, anchors were a lesson in themselves.

"You've got to make sure you take the right anchor for the right boat. Never head out into the lake without your anchors. Weather changes, engines stall, and things get rough if the wind picks up. You may think you will spend all day out there, but things can change quickly on the lake. When the wind picks up, if you've got nothing to slow you down, it will blow you into someone's dock or boat. You can get hurt."

Looking squarely into my eyes, he demanded, "Buddy, you got that?"

In the boathouse was an assortment of anchors. Small ball and mushroom anchors sat in one corner of that dwelling. In another corner, two heavy scoop anchors laid against the wall.

The scoop anchors with broad hooks were heavy and clunky. When cast overboard, the anchors dug deep into the bottom of the lake, stabilizing the boat above from the winds that blew. They were perfect for the heavy old MaryAnne.

The next summer, a promotion in personal boating status occurred. Grandpa desired that his oldest grandson enjoy the opportunity to captain the MaryAnne. It marked another proud, confident building moment. After several lessons, grandpa stood confident in his oldest grandson's ability to captain the family boat.

⚓ Which Anchor?

One morning, a cruise up and down the lake was organized. Intending to spend the entire day on the lake, we loaded the MaryAnne with coolers of drinks, food, snacks, and fishing gear as we prepared to launch.

Entering the boathouse, I reached for the scoop anchor. The old steel weight proved heavy and cumbersome. On a bright, cloudless sunny morning, what might be the actual need for such an old heavy burdensome thing? Opting for two much smaller mushroom anchors, we finished loading and shoved off.

Coasting down the South-West side of the Lake, we reached Woods Bay. In this bay, surrounded by high hills and trees, the water stood still as glass. Fishing most of the morning, the skies began to darkened near the afternoon. It was time to return to the cabin.

We headed out of the bay through two small channels into the wide-open waters of Roosevelt Lake. Leaving the calm waters of the bay for the choppy waves of the lake concerned everyone. Then, as the winds picked up, crashing waves slammed into the boat.

In this long lake of over 8 miles, our journey was slow in the driving wind. Then the rain came, pounding so hard and furious that visibility became nonexistent. The MaryAnne crashed against the breakers of the water, hurling us all about.

Then it happened. A small sputter, and nothing. That old motor died. As the wind blew us into an indiscernible direction, I kept pushing the electric start button, trying to start the old motor. Nothing. The wind drove us in a direction impossible to discern. Quickly, we cast both anchors overboard. Problem.

While two small 5-pound Mushroom anchors usually proved adequate for grandpa's much lighter boat, they fell far short of what the MaryAnne needed. Winds and waves rocked the boat, driving us towards an unseeable shoreline.

Then it happened. Crash! The MaryAnne crashed into a 30-foot dock protruding from the shoreline. We grabbed onto the dock, tied down the boat, and rode out the storm.

Ninety minutes later, on a glass calm lake, grandpa approached in his boat. Starting the MaryAnne after several hours, we limped the injured old lady back to the cabin. The next morning grandpa asked for a conversation.

"Buddy, remember what I told you about anchors?" Bowing in shame, I replied, "Yes, sorry, grandpa." He continued, "I am glad you, your brothers, and sisters are ok. That is the key thing. But great-grandma's boat is pretty banged up. That's your fault. You didn't follow my instructions about anchors. Right?"

Acknowledging my discernable error became a lifelong lesson still with me over forty years later. My error cost grandpa time and money repairing the boat before handing it over to his sister.

⚓ Choosing Your Anchors

The question each worker must ask themselves is, "What anchors will I choose to steady my life, family, relationships, and ministry to enable me to endure the challenges which most certainly lay ahead?"

Looking back over forty years of missionary and pastoral life, it is—to me—one of the most important questions you'll ever ask and seek to answer.

Dangerous Anchors

In 1883, in Glasgow, Scotland, they launched the newly constructed SS Daphne into open waters. She sank almost immediately, drowning 124 workers on board. The cause of the sinking laid within its anchors.

Around 200 workmen were on board as they launched the ship. The workers intended to fit the 450-ton Daphne as soon as she was properly afloat. As per the usual practice, anchors were attached by cables to each side of the ship providing stabilization of the vessel as it slipped into the waters.

As the Daphne lurched into the river, the anchors failed to stop the ship's forward progress. The starboard anchor moved only 6-7 yards, but the port anchor dragged 60 yards. The currents of the river caught the Daphne flipping it over onto its port side. She sank in deep water. Around 120 died, including many young apprentice boys, some of whose relatives watched the ceremony from shore.[15]

"The cause of the disaster was reported to be little initial stability combined with too much loose gear and too many people aboard."[16] After the disaster, laws changed reducing the number of workers onboard to only those necessary for mooring and stabilizing a vessel. They raised, repaired, and renamed SS Daphne, the Rose.[17]

As with the Daphne, many missionaries anchor their souls poorly. Weights, thought to secure, don't prevent their soul's drift towards the rocky grounds of doubt and despair. Life's shorelines are strewn with the wreckages of poorly anchored missionary souls.

Focalism

While anchoring often conjures up heavy items dropped overboard from tethered boats, it also refers to human emotion.

Anchoring or *Focalism* is a term used in psychology to describe a common cognitive human tendency to rely too heavily, or "anchor," oneself upon a single trait or piece of information when making decisions.[18] In Anchoring, people decide based upon a single conversation, experience, or initial piece of information.

For example, a cross-cultural worker can anchor their expectations and plans in their new venture based upon their short-term mission trips to the field. He or she might expect their newest experience to resemble those short few days when missionaries catered to their every need during their visit.

For missionaries, it's easy to fall into the trap of focalism: what was yesterday will be today, and what is today must be tomorrow. This assumes that my home, vehicles, children's school, ministry, finances, and church will continue as expected. All will be as it was.

Yes, it's good—and necessary—to settle into your new lifestyle upon arriving to the field. Make your new country home. Get comfortable. Climatize. Learn the language. Enjoy the people. But understand that situations arise which can upend your best plans and preparations. Don't anchor yourself so deeply in your today that it must be your tomorrow. This disposition is not dependable.

Missionary life is often an existence of constant flux and transition. Focalism focuses too much upon a single ideal or experience in a worker's life.

For example, it is common to hear from new missionaries their dissatisfaction with the first team or couple with which they served. When suggesting any consideration of another team, often a vigorous negative response follows.

"No, I will never work with another missionary because of my experience with the last one."

One unpleasant experience, often a reciprocal mutual failure by both parties, becomes the single experience the worker bases all future decisions to join any team. This is focalism. Battling this tendency requires our minds and souls be anchored to a secure source.

⚓ Dependable Anchors

If we are to endure the storms coming our way, we need reliable anchoring. Anchors that fix our souls upon something other than a negative moment, unpleasant station of ministry, location, or achievement.

Perhaps you're experiencing incredible challenges right now. Maybe the failure of health, betrayal, job loss, income depreciation, or fractured relationships; biospheres full of unrest. Your soul sways in the buffetings. At any moment, the swells may breech your hull.

You ask, "What should I do?"

Answer, "Check and make sure of your anchors."

There are only a few dependable anchors that promise not to fail us. Promises that are never broken. Fix yourself to these:

God himself. I love verse twenty-six of Psalm 73. It continually strengthens my soul. It is an anchoring verse of the truth of God's faithfulness and person.

"My flesh and my heart fail; But God is the strength of my heart and my portion forever."

NKJV

For many of us, our strength fails. Our hope diminishes in the face of a prolonged grinding down that often occurs in missionary life. This is a reality that few workers ever mention to their supporters or churches back home.

I sat in a meeting recently while a missionary couple shared their harrowing ordeal before a group of pastors. The experience left them in a state of depression and doubt. They asked for prayer and sat down.

The keynote speaker went to the front and opened with a fifteen minute self-inflating introduction on how he'd never struggled with depression, doubt, or ever a thought of quitting.

I thought, "You're a liar or the most impressive person I've ever met."

One thing was certain that morning. That missionary couple would leave without the aid or comfort of the Bible admonition to bear one another's burdens.

After the sessions, we gathered for lunch in the church gym. Upon my entry, the missionary couple sat alone. I asked to sit with them.

Sitting down, our eyes met. What I saw in the couple's eyes was defeat. I will never forget their look of abandonment. All the while, that speaker sat at the table behind us, laughing and joking with friends, unaware of the shaming and damage he caused.

I offered, "I'm sorry about those words—bobbing my head back towards the man—he just doesn't understand missionaries."

Then the wife spoke up. "They don't care, so why should we." They resigned from missionary service later that year.

Missionary, unless God be your rock and anchor, you're destined to crash upon the destitute shores of discontent. People will almost always fail you. I will fail you. You will fail. We fail each other. Few mean to do so, but it's within our nature to look more towards ourselves than others.

God is the One we must always look to.

Jesus Christ. He is our only perfect example. Jesus told his disciples in John 14:6 that he was, "The way, the truth, and the light." As cross-cultural workers, it is good for us to remember that not only is Jesus our Way of salvation, but he is also the way by which we process life.

His way is truth. The truth that embodies Christ brings us light. Jesus' light shines into every situation, showing us the truthfulness of how to live and move forward in every step of our life.

When faced with life changing situations, look to Jesus for the way. Ask for God to show you truth through his son. To light your course when all seems lost, or an irrevocable shift changes the course of your life.

Read the words of Jesus often. In them, he gives us the truth of his person and the way we are to live in every circumstance. Jesus is our anchor that never fails. As the old hymn proclaims,

> We have an anchor that keeps the soul,
> Steadfast and sure while the billows roll,
> Fastened to the Rock which cannot move,
> Grounded firm and deep in the Savior's love.[19]

The Holy Spirit. God's sweet Spirit is the wind that leads and guides us. Seek the Holy Spirit often in your every step. Then wait upon God's Spirit to guide and fill you.

This is a truth God gives us, "And this hope will not lead to disappointment. For we know how dearly God loves us, because he has given us the Holy Spirit to fill our hearts with his love." Romans 5:5

The Word of God. Throughout the many seminars, conferences, and classes I've attended over the decades, the Bible—God's Word—remains my most reliable source of guidance and stability. Even in the most tumultuous of struggles, God's Word soothes and comforts, reinforces, secures, and steadies my soul.

Here are two verses from Habakkuk that encourage me often:

Even though the fig trees have no blossoms, and there are no grapes on the vines; even though the olive crop fails, and the fields lie empty and barren;

39

even though the flocks die in the fields, and the cattle barns are empty, yet I will rejoice in the LORD! I will be joyful in the God of my salvation!

Habakkuk 3:17-18

Regardless of the situation, I will rejoice in the LORD. And—here's the challenging part—be joyful in God, no matter what.

These four anchors, God's Person, Jesus' sacrifice and example, the precious Holy Spirit's guidance, and the directing Word of God will secure you in any storm.

⚓ Secondary Anchors

Every missionary needs financial backing for their voyage—a church, organization, and supporters behind them. I like to call these secondary anchors. While necessary, they are not the chief mast of our souls providing the stability we need.

Friendships and partnerships provide necessary outfitting and rigging for our journey, but we can only view them as secondary anchors. Sometimes these anchors prove unreliable. Too much confidence in them produces anxiety and stress when they fail.

During my years in South Africa, we witnessed many South African missionaries raise their support from South African churches and supporters before leaving for the mission field. Upon returning home, they often shared of their financial woes.

Some churches changed pastors. Their missions emphasis altered, reducing the amount of monthly contributions the missionary received. All South African missionaries struggled with the plunging devaluation of the South African Rand.

Missionaries found it difficult to survive financially as the Rand purchased fewer and fewer units in their local currencies. It forced many to either return

40

home permanently or secure secular work in the countries they lived to support themselves.

Another example is that of SBC missionary dilemma. In 2015, under severe financial duress, the Southern Baptist Convention offered 983 of their Missionaries a Voluntary Retirement Initiative.[20] With the International Mission Board reeling from budget shortfalls, they decided that the only way to remedy the situation was to let go nearly 1,000 of their missionaries. Missionaries who through the IMB enjoyed funding at an average of $4,300 per month through the Cooperative Program and Lottie Moon Christmas offering.[21]

"Live every day like you will stay forever, but may need to leave tomorrow," never proved truer. Within only a few short months of notification, workers who lived in their fields of service for decades saw their lives irrevocably altered as they left the field forever.

When COVID-19 hit in 2020, many missionaries told of losing contributions from individuals who supported them. One missionary shared that within a few months he'd lost $1,200.00 a month in regular contributions.

I like a quote from the Greek philosopher Epictetus. Epictetus was born a slave. He gained his freedom after the death of the Roman Emperor Nero. As a Greek Speaking Stoic Philosopher, he was banished from Rome when Emperor Domitian cast all philosophers out of the city, along with murdering thousands of Christians.

He traveled to Nilopolis in Greece, where he founded his own philosophy school. Epictetus taught philosophy as a way of life and practice rather than theoretical engagement. He maintained the only external event controllable is our response to what happens to us.[22]

When putting one's hope in a single instance of life, he nailed it, *"Neither should a ship rely on one small anchor, nor should life rest on a single hope."*

⚓ Chose an Anchor that Will Secure Your Soul

Anchors provide stability in stormy waters. Or they can cause a ship to list, if incorrectly applied, dragging it down to the water's bottom. Only an appropriate anchor, properly secured, can steady our souls throughout our cross-cultural journeys from beginning to end.

Therefore, we who have fled to him for refuge can have great confidence as we hold to the hope that lies before us. This hope is a strong and trustworthy anchor for our souls.

Hebrews 6:18b-19a

 Sail On

Think about your anchors — that which you base your future expectations upon. Write them down. Be gut-wrenching honest with yourself.

Then ask, "Are these anchors reliable? Will they hold me through the gales of life and ministry?" Check the box either *Yes* or *No*.

Anchor	Reliable?
1. _____	Yes ____ No ____
2. _____	Yes ____ No ____
3. _____	Yes ____ No ____
4. _____	Yes ____ No ____
5. _____	Yes ____ No ____
6. _____	Yes ____ No ____
7. _____	Yes ____ No ____

True North

So God has given both his promise and his oath. These two things are unchangeable because it is impossible for God to lie.

Therefore, we who have fled to him for refuge can *have great confidence as we hold to the hope* that lies before us.

This *hope is a strong and trustworthy **anchor** for our souls.*

It leads us through the curtain into God's inner sanctuary. Jesus has already gone in there for us.

Hebrews 6:18-20a

 Light House

God made an oath to Abraham. Genesis 17:1-8, Hebrews 6:17, 7:21; Psalms 110:4

That oath was a promise to bless and multiply Abraham's heirs. We are also recipients of God's blessing upon Abraham's life. Through Jesus Christ, we are beneficiaries of this oath. Gal. 3:29

God's integrity assures us He will never go back upon the oath he made to Abraham. Jesus secures this guarantee for us. God will provide for our every need.

43

Be blessed because you are blessed.

Now, can you sing about that?

Or, maybe even smile!

Survival Tip #4

Learn to Practice the Presence of God

*I must first have the sense of God's possession of me
before I can have the sense of
His presence with me.*

— Watchman Nee, The Normal Christian Life

THE GOVERNOR, CELEBRITIES, DIGNITARIES, CLERGY, and business people gathered for the Minnesota Prayer Breakfast at the Hilton Hotel in downtown Minneapolis, Minnesota. The ceremony began with an invocation.

"May your presence be with us this morning, and in the coming days…"
A notion pierced my mind while standing there among hundreds of people with my eyes closed.

"Is not God's presence always with us?"

Disengaged from the entreaty, I thought, "God, you are always present in our lives. Help us sense your continual presence. Help each one here this morning to discipline ourselves to practice your presence in every moment of every day."

God is everywhere all the time. Theological training and Bible studies teach us this is so. With the nod of our heads we affirm this truth, but our hearts often turn away from a sense of God's presence in busy self-directed aspirations and activities.

There is no more important principle than this Spiritual Survival Tip: *God is always present; learn to practice sensing his presence.*

For the Bible Tells Me So...

In John 14:6, Jesus told his disciples he was the way, the truth, and the life. He insisted that no one came to his Father but through him. In a letter to Christians at Ephesus, Paul explained that because of what Christ did for us, we always have access to the Father. Ephesians 2:18

Hebrews reinforces this beautiful truth. Because of Jesus' finished work on the cross, we can confidently approach God, receiving grace, favor, and mercy—kindness—in our time of need. Hebrews 4:16

The writer of Hebrew encourages us to learn contentment by remembering that God never leaves or quits on us. God is always present with us. Hebrews 13:5

Through Jesus Christ, we enjoy immediate and continual access to God. God is omnipresent—present everywhere at the same time; ubiquitous, boundless, and infinite. *We know this. We just don't practice God's presence outside our religious activities.*

Often overlooked is God's presence in us, around us, and through us because we get wrapped up in the sufficiency of our own plans and initiatives.

We tend to move toward God when sensing a lack of control. It's then we need God to get us back on course with our health, plans, or programs.

The ideal for the Christian worker is to sense God's presence at all times. An awareness in the soul that senses God presence both in the mundane and momentous events of life.

Learning to Practice God's Presence

Practicing God's presence is a simple concept of *understanding that God is current every day, every moment, every second, and during every activity of our lives.*

Practicing this truth is a consciousness of knowing of God throughout each day.[23] Fairly basic, right?

While elementary, it's perhaps the most neglected practice of many missionaries.

Simon Dube

Shortly after our arrival in South Africa years ago, a neighbor offered to introduce me to a language helper. We left Ladysmith, a small modern city with a European atmosphere, and headed out to the rural townships and villages where Zulu people lived.

On the blacktop road, brick houses and factories quickly changed into mud huts and with small cement block houses dotting the jagged hills. Turning off the road unto a dirt path, we began making our way down through the village. Young Zulu boys played soccer with bare feet on fields of dirt. Others attended to goats and cattle.

Driving down through the boulder-strewn terrain and crossing over a small sully creek, we arrived at Simon Dube's house. He met us upon our arrival and invited us into his home.

47

It rained that day, and water dripped into the house from a dozen places. The corrugated metal sheets Simon used to roof his home were old, rusted, and filled with hundreds of holes.

Simon's wife filled the potbelly stove with wood. Once the water came to a boil, she placed three plastic cups on the table in front of us along with instant coffee, powdered creamer, and sugar.

Then Simon—sipping his coffee—asked me a most unexpected question.

"What do you desire to bring my people that we truly need?"

A host of answers came out of my mouth, reflecting the aspirations of a young missionary's desire for ministry among the Zulu people.

After listening for thirty minutes, he set his second cup of coffee down, and exhaled a deep breath of hesitation. He looked up into the air and began speaking in a mixture of English and Zulu.

"All those things you speak of are good, but... we don't need those plans or ideas out here. What we need is *uNkulukulu ukuba khona nathi*."

Those four words in the Zulu language translate, *God to be here with us*. He repeated several times that the need of his people was, "*God to be here with us*."

That day, the old Zulu man taught me more about missiology—*God to be here with us*—than all my studies and thoughts combined. God's presence was the goal. Not that God wasn't already with us, the old man concluded, it was just that we needed a renewed sense of Emmanuel — God is with us.

> We need a renewed sense of Emmanuel – God is with us.

Wow! That day proved humbling for me; a much-needed chastening to correct a young, proud attitude of condescension. A mindset too often typical of western missionaries.

Truth was that the old Zulu man knew God well. An everywhereness of God he learned to embrace during his years in the POW camps of Nazi Germany during the WWII.

They captured Simon in Libya during the North African campaign against Rommel and the Axis forces in 1940. As a POW, he suffered immensely under German and Italian guards. It was in those camps he perceived an inexplicable presence of God while experiencing beatings, deprivations, and starvation.

Simon was seventy when I met him in in 1986. Sitting with him that day, he looked at a young twenty-eight-year-old white missionary and asked, "Can you help me bring my people to God?"

Looking Back

Looking back over missionary years and careers—including my own—it's unfortunate the many times that our emotions acted as if God didn't exist at all. Actions that suggested more of a Christian agnosticism than an embracing of an ever-present God. When we react in adversity and hardship by throwing up of the hands and crying, *"What's the use?"*

A thought process of, "It's like God isn't even on board with what I'm trying to do here."

As a missionary once shared, "Nothing is working out. I guess God is finished with me."

It's a false narrative. The words of a downcast soul may say so, but it doesn't change the ever-presence of God. He is never finished with us. He is always present, and we must sense it to be so.

And it also flies in the face of Paul's words to the believers in the ancient city of Philippi, "And I am certain that God, who began the good work within you, will continue his work until it is finally finished on the day when Christ Jesus returns." Philippians 1:6

Once while talking with Kathy at our favorite coffee shop—Wimpy's—in Ladysmith, South Africa, my words of discouragement carried to ears of those at the next table. Looking down at my coffee, whining about a challenge we faced, I felt a presence at the end of the booth.

Looking up, a young, well-dressed thin Indian man pointed his finger at me and said in King James English, "Sir, remember this! My God will never leave thee or forsake thee!" With that, he walked out the door. I never saw him again.

God is always present, and we must sense it to be so.

Here's the thing. Unless you learn to practice the discipline of sensing God's presence consciously in your life—no matter how menial or significant the moment—emotions will push you toward unsteady waters of doubt, skepticism, and apathy.

I see it all the time. Missionaries attempting spiritual tasks of making disciples without the slightest hint of God's presence in their efforts and work. Oh, they know God is with them theologically. They just don't grasp it experientially. They possess little sense that *God is here right now at this very moment.*

God's Presence—Our Doubts

One facet about my missionary life where I'd like a do-over is to make my service more about God and less about me. A quest that life is more a moment by moment faith-walk with God than a busy pursuit of doing stuff for God.

Ever taken a tour on a cruise ship? When you arrive at the ship, your asked to surrender your luggage to a porter. This is someone you've never met. Then a crew member—another stranger—will help you find your cabin. As you settle in, the ship leaves port. There's one constant that puts you at ease. Even though you've not seen one—a *captain* is on board.

Now, you never saw your captain, did you? But your confidence in a captain's presence allayed any apprehensions. That unseen presence along with a crew providing for your every need during the voyage brought a sense of ease and expectation.

God's presence is our confidence. Faith tells me I can feel God, sense God, and know God. Faith is the portal.

Anyone who wants to come to him must **believe that God exists** and that he **rewards** those who **sincerely seek him**.

Hebrews 11:6b Emphasis Mine

Faith earnestly seeks after God's presence—a presence that rewards the seeker. From the most unpleasant tasks, largest trials, and greatest achievements of life, faith sees God. In our boredoms, trials, and victories, faith discerns God is with me. This offers an inner peace. *God's got this under control. Emmanuel, God with us.*

Yet, there's something about many of us—workers, leaders, and shepherds—that allows us to drift away from the Creator's presence into our own sufficiency and self-worth. Our inclination is to enjoy sailing the waters of self-confidence and performance. In this, we gain a sense of accomplishment when performing our actions for God, not sensing a nearness to God.

The busyness of Christian activities, undesired duties, weak spiritual disciples, ego soothing events, traumatic experiences, and a drive to reach our aspirations turns our spiritual focuses away from God. Self distances us away from the very Captain who devotedly stands at the helm, guiding us in the stormiest of waters.

How Well Do You Know Your Captain?

How well do you really know your Captain? Asking this survival tip question at a missionary retreat in Central America before 300 missionaries, a middle 30s missionary who just arrived on the field expressed a predictable response.

"Well, yah… God. We all know that."

My response, "Yes, we all know that, but do we all sense that right now?"

The zest that filled the recent arrival's face turned blank, and said, "Well, honestly, I… don't know."

"How many of you," I asked, "Feel the same way. Right here. Right now."

Many hands went up that morning.

Until we believe it, sense it, and grasp that God is our very present help in times of trouble, [24] we will flounder in our seas of service.

Let me give you another example of what I'm trying to get across here.

Blessing Myself on a Nail

It reminds me of something I experienced as a young catholic boy while attending catechism classes at St. Anne's Catholic Church in North Minneapolis. A priest—Father Freed—brought a challenging lesson one morning to our catechism class—a lesson still remembered fifty years later.

His teaching was on "The Importance of the Sign of the Cross." Little did we know that the lesson already began before Father Freed entered the room that morning.

As each student entered the room, they stopped at the font… or stoup—a bowl of holy water—and dipped their fingers into the bowl. Pulling our fingers wet with holy water from the bowl, we each made the sign of the cross upon our forehead, heart, and shoulders saying, "In the name of the Father, the Son, and the Holy Spirit." Making the sign of the cross acknowledges that God became one for us.[25] It is a holy function of millions of Catholics.

Father Freed soon entered the classroom and began with a question.

"Students, when entering the class today did you all bless yourselves with holy water by making the sign of the cross?"

Acknowledging that we'd done so, Father Freed protested, "Are you sure?"

We all affirmed that we blessed ourselves upon entering the room.

"I don't think so," continued Father Freed, "I'd like you to break into groups and discuss what the sign of the cross means."

In each group, we chose a spokesperson to explain the practice of blessing one's self with holy water through the sign of the cross.

Father Freed asked again. "Tell me now, how did you bless yourselves with the sign of the cross through holy water this morning."

Each spokesperson gave a quick response. Yet Father Freed objected again.

"There is something still missing here, and I tell you that none of you fully performed the sign of the cross this morning."

Walking over to the door frame, he pointed to the stoup that held the holy water. Except, there was no stoup on the wall that day. So accustom to the bowl of holy water dangling from aside the door, not one of us noticed that only a small nail protruded from the door frame.

Father Freed smiled and said, "Students, you all blessed yourselves on a nail this morning."

Then he chuckled, "You received a nail-blessing."

The religious practice of dipping our fingers into the bowl and blessing ourselves with holy water through the sign of the cross became so perfunctory that it held little significance. So little, that in assenting to its importance not one of us noting is absence.

We, as missionaries, do this all the time with God. While in the routines of life, we hardly give God a thought, blessing ourselves on a nail of activity, accomplishments, and personal pursuits.

God's Presence in Mundanities

Somewhere in the life and work of our calling we lose touch with God as other passions consume our energies. We bless ourselves on a nail of perfunctory activity rather than God's presence.

In the banal duties life assigns us, we don't see God. "This isn't worth my time," one may say. Scripture argues, "Whatever you do, do it all for the glory of God." [26]

My grandpa Mingo served on a ship in WWII as a Seaman 2nd Class Machinist, deep in the haul of a ship. Once he mentioned that, the machinists could only stand topside on deck a few hours a day. He said, "When at sea, our job was to keep the engines running. And that's exactly what we did down in the hole."

The entire crew from captain to deckhand depended upon those machinists deep in the haul of that ship, making sure the vessel remained operational.

"This is not worthy of my time!" we might say.

When asked to perform a menial task, perhaps there is a feeling of, "This is below my worthiness? It's not worth my time?" Yet sensing God's presence helps turn that which is tedious and humble into an act of worship. An act that well pleases the Father.

God's Presence in the Momentous

So too, in monumental events and achievements of life, God is with us. Sensing God in our accomplishments and triumphs keeps us from filling with pride, hoarding recognition for ourselves to the exclusion of God's provision in our personal success.

When experiencing significant achievements, consciously perceiving God enables us to resist pride's enticement of entitlement towards the excluding of others. Sensing God's presence appreciates that our triumphs never come from our sole efforts alone.

Practicing God's presence helps us obey the Shema, 'You must love the LORD your God with all your heart, all your soul, and all your mind.' Matthew 22:37

When the Storms Blow

There's a lot of trauma in this world. Unfortunately as a cross-cultural worker you will experience trauma too. Perhaps you'll experience it first hand as a victim. Maybe the suffering of others will impact you causing vicarious trauma within you. Trauma affects the soul.

> Unless you hunger for a sense of God's presence, your soul is destined for shipwreck.

As one who served over twenty years in Africa, and survived the later ravages of PTSD, I share with absolute confidence that: *unless you hunger for a sense of God's presence, your soul is destined for shipwreck.*

When storms approach, as they undoubtedly will, you'll benefit little by simply believing you're on a mission for God. Neither will the mere adventure of your calling sustain you indefinitely.

When trials grind you down, the floods of depression, doubt, or despair pound your soul's hull, only the Great I AM can steady you towards safe harbor.

A sense that:

God, You are present right here, right now. There are no accidents in You. Everything happening here furthers Your purpose and plans in my life. You are with me. You will never leave me. God, you are my Emmanuel.

Before turbulent waves crack your hull–Emmanuel
Before the taste for the adventure fades–Emmanuel
Before the need of people overwhelms you–Emmanuel
Before funds and resources evaporate–Emmanuel
Before reports, policies, and meetings–Emmanuel
Before news and press reports–Emmanuel
Before social media–Emmanuel
Before your first departure for the field–Emmanuel
Before your next furlough–Emmanuel
Before your next transition of life–Emmanuel

In momentous achievements–Emmanuel
In beginnings and endings–Emmanuel

God's Presence Our Sustenance

Paul Bunyan, an 17th English writer and Puritan preacher, who refused when ordered to stop preaching, spent twelve years in prison. During those arduous years, he wrote the famed Christian allegory *Pilgrim's Progress*. Concerning his prison experience, he wrote:

> *God has put me in a place where I can no longer live on my work. I can no longer live on my family... on my friends... on my pleasures... [or,] on my ministry. I have to live on God, who is invisible."* [27]

 Sail On

When is the last time you remember sensing God's presence? When you felt— experienced—that God is your Emmanuel—God with me? Take some time. Think about it. Write it down.

_____

_____

_____

In what setting do you feel closest to God? What's your special place?

_____

_____

_____

When's the last time you met with God at that special place?

_____

_____

 True North

You will show me the way of life, granting me the joy of your presence and the pleasures of living with you forever.

Psalm 16:11

His purpose was for the nations to seek after God and perhaps feel their way toward him and find him—though he is not far from any one of us. For in him we live and move and exist.

Acts 17:27-28

Yet I am always with you; you hold me by my right hand. You guide me with your counsel, and afterward you will take me into glory.

Psalms 73:23-24

Where can I flee from your presence? If I go up to the heavens, you are there; if I make my bed in the depths, you are there.

Psalm 139:7-8 NIV

57

Light House

Cultivate a practice of walking consciously with God. In each moment of every circumstance, in every day, think, "Emmanuel, God You are with me."

Hey, have you smiled today?

Survival Tip #5

Master the Bible as Your Compass

THEY STILL USE COMPASSES ON ships today. Take, for example, the gyrocompass which functions unhampered by the earth's magnetic field. It's used to find the True North position to provide a stable directional course.

The magnetic compass is used to plot out a ship's course for a voyage. Without the help of compasses and GPS systems, guideless vessels would run aground or cruise aimlessly from one unknown place to another.

During your missionary journey, you'll experience a barrage of human experiences and physical conditions. Here's a question best answered now, "What will guide you on your journey?"

When I was fourteen, my mother sent me off to summer camp along with my brother. Camp Voyageur up in Willow River, Minnesota, provided a wilderness retreat where we learned a variety of basic outdoor survival skills. One lesson was on the use of a compass. The instructor often rehearsed, "Boys, once you find your True North, you'll know where to go."

The Bible is that spiritual compass finding our true North in *attitudes* and *actions*. As a cross-cultural worker, you'll need the Bible's stability in plotting out interactions with those around you and a stable directional course in your relationship with God.

> **You need to follow the Bible's stability in your interaction with others.**

This morning amid the COVID-19 world pandemic, fifty missionaries met online during four different Zoom Conferences. I was a part of each of those conferences. Each missionary took a few minutes to share their struggles. For many, confinement to their homes proved their greatest challenge.

With no ability to meet with their church leaders and people during imposed lockdowns, every missionary—without exception—cited a particular passage of Scripture that encouraged them. Together, we bathed each other in the Bible.

Yet Bible reading is often a neglected discipline in a missionary's life. The demands of the work, needs of the people, and drive to achieve frequently clutters the soul with busyness.

While canvasing members of several global workers' care networks, I asked this question. *What is the most neglected spiritual principle among Christian cross-cultural workers?* Several themes emerged. Margie, a 15-year cross-cultural veteran, shared the most glaring deficit of missionaries today:

Hi Don, in response to your question as to neglected spiritual principles and disciplines of missionaries, I would say… in 2021… Sadly, a major insidious neglect is the Bible. Reading, studying, saturating, memorizing, meditating and applying it to the missionary's life.

Theology and Biblical literacy is my number one observation of what "makes or breaks" a person in long term, effective, cross-cultural ministry.

Dozens of global member care workers echoed Margie's response. Missionaries spent little time in God's Word. Often neglected for the work's sake, a typical response was, "I just can't find the time."

Another caregiver noted that often today's missionaries arrive on the field possessing little Bible literacy. It's that simple. Missionaries who are sent to serve set their compasses towards other markers outside of the Bible.

Scripture is the only tangible constant we can hold in our hands that will guide us through the rough seas of relationship and ministry.

Other deficits common among workers related directly to a lack of Bible comprehension and the skill to apply biblical truths to their behavior and attitudes. Such as:

⊘ Kindness

If you're new to missions, I'll let you in on a secret. Missionaries often struggle to get along with each other. I can't tell you the number of missionaries resigning who cite conflict with another missionary as their reason for leaving the field. This was true among the pioneer missionaries of the 18th Century, as it's true today.

Much of the trouble missionaries suffer among themselves exists from a failure to obey Scriptural guidance in relationship building. Most conflicts would cease if the very book we claim to believe we'd just follow.

Fellow care providers shared the unkindness that often accompanies missionaries at odds with each other. One care worker declared, "Unfortunately, Don, some of the most unkind people I've ever met are missionaries."

Another example stands out to me. Asked to assist a group of missionaries in a dispute with each other, I traveled to their country. Spending a week among those missionaries revealed the core of the conflict.

A senior retiring missionary recruited a new missionary and his wife to oversee the Mission Hospital. Upon arriving, they immediately took control.

Other long-term missionaries at the premises knew nothing about the succession of power.

The new missionary, before learning the language, immediately changed personnel. Workers engaged with the hospital, who'd spent years serving there became alarmed.

The conflict reached its Dunkirk when the new missionary fired the director. An elderly indigenous man who'd served over ten years. When he refused to leave, the new missionary illegally evicted him off the premises.

The dismissed director called the authorities, and as the police arrived, they walked into a group of missionaries cursing and yelling at each other.

Are you kidding me?

Can you imagine, here are the national people—citizens—witnessing a group of foreigners, missionaries no less, involved in such behavior?

Embrace the Bible's compass, pointing you towards kindness. It's tough out there in the field, the voyage of can produce a hard, gruff person. Those who confront at every issue, choosing combat over community.

I just spoke with a CEO of a Missionary Care organization in Central American. Enquiring about his spiritual health, he replied, "I'm doing well, but it's getting a little chippy out here with some of these missionaries. You know…"

Looking on the organization's Facebook page, a battle of words was in full array between several missionaries over approaches in dealing with the COVID-19 crisis.

In my own confession of falling short here, once in a village just outside of Ladysmith, South Africa, a few missionaries held a softball clinic. Over thirty Zulu teenagers attended.

As we started, another missionary irritated me immensely. My focus was on teaching the game of softball. His emphasis was to have fun, even if it meant not learning the fundamentals of the game.

My irritation showed as I chewed the younger missionary out for not following the rules that I—a seasoned, veteran, cross-cultural worker—deemed necessary. The young Zulu teens observed the conflict, which was pretty much one-sided.

After we all packed up, the younger missionary came to me with a wrapped Christmas gift. It was December. The gift humbled me. And later, in my quiet time, a Scripture pierced my soul:

> Instead, *be kind to each other, tenderhearted*, forgiving one another, just as God through Christ has forgiven you.

> Ephesians 4:32

⊘ Forgiving

That younger missionary willingly forgave me, and our friendship deepened over the years. We enjoyed many opportunities to work together advancing the Gospel throughout the Zulu Kingdom in Natal.

Missionary conflict is rarely the genuine reason workers leave their fields. The cause of such mutinies is more of an unwillingness to grasp and follow our biblical compass that guides us through turbulent waters of relational conflict.

> Make allowance for each other's faults, and forgive anyone who offends you. Remember, *the Lord forgave you, so you must forgive others.*

> Colossians 3:13 Emphasis Mine

What does the Bible say about resolving conflict in relationships? Be kind. Be forgiving. If you want to resolve disputes, clear the deck of your animosities and bitterness. Follow your Captain's orders:

> If you forgive those who sin against you, your heavenly Father will forgive you. But *if you refuse to forgive others, your Father will not forgive your sins.*   Matthew 6:14-15 Emphasis Mine

But when you are praying, first *forgive anyone you are holding a grudge against, so that your Father in heaven will forgive your sins, too.*

Mark 11:25 Emphasis Mine

When I look back on my years in South Africa, how much more might our teams have affected lives and ministries if each missionary realized:

- We all have faults.
- We need to be patient with each other.
- We all need forgiveness.
- God forgave me for all of my faults.
- God expects—no, demands—I forgive others for their faults.

We make allowances for other team member's flaws, because:

1. Our Compass—the Bible—instructs it.
2. Our Savior—the Captain—demands it.
3. Our Journey—the Destination—depends upon it.

⊘ Hopefulness

It's unavoidable. In your missionary ministry, you'll drift into despondency at times. Paul—the Father of Missions—found himself in these waters many times.

When we arrived in Macedonia, there was no rest for us. We faced conflict from every direction, with battles on the outside and fear on the inside.

2 Corinthians 7:5

We think you ought to know, dear brothers and sisters, about the trouble we went through in the province of Asia. We were crushed and overwhelmed beyond our ability to endure, and we thought we would never live through it.

2 Corinthians 1:8

There are hosts of reasons for this. Many workers who've spent a smidgen of time out on the field battle with depression and despair. Study even the great missionaries of the past, and you'll discover this to be true too.

Adoniram Judson—nineteenth-century missionary to Burma—suffered immense losses during his missionary career.[28]

Judson's and his first wife, Ann, married February 5, 1812. They left for Burma that same month. During their years together on the field, Ann gave birth to 3 children.

The first baby, nameless, was born dead just as they sailed from India to Burma. Their second child, Roger Williams Judson, lived 17 months and died.

In 1824 to 1825, Judson spent seventeen months in a Burmese prison. They gave little food to him. They bound his feet to a large bamboo pole, his hands to another, and at night his feet lifted higher than his head.

Ann, his heroic wife, brought little bits of food to him, although she and the baby were near death, and both would die soon after Judson's release from prison.[29]

Their third child, Maria Elizabeth Butterworth Judson having outlived her mother by six months, died at two years of age.[30] After Ann's death, Adoniram sank into a deep depression. He moved himself to the heart of a tiger-infested jungle to live alone in a hut. Judson doubted his call and occasionally contemplated suicide.[31]

How did he survive such trials? He wrote, "If I had not felt certain that every additional trial was ordered by infinite love and mercy, I could not have survived my accumulated sufferings."[32]

Judson wrote to missionary candidates in 1832:

Remember, a large proportion of those who come out on a mission to the East die within five years after leaving their native land. Walk softly, therefore; death is narrowly watching your steps.[33]

Lottie Moon (December 12, 1840–December 24, 1912) was the famed female missionary to China. She was perhaps the first single female missionary of the modern missionary movement. Constantly badgered by both missionaries and the Chinese, they often questioned her singleness and asked if she'd ever been in love. She often replied, "Yes, but God had first claim on my life, and since the two conflicted, there could be no question about the result."[34]

When Chinese villagers continually pressed her why she never married, she replied, "Because I'm afraid of how mothers-in-laws might beat me." This often brought a smile from villagers and defused the confrontation.

She excelled in literature and languages; she learned Greek, Latin, Italian, French, and Spanish. By the time she completed her master's degree, some considered her to be the best-educated woman in the South.[35]

Lottie achieved many victories. First, she gained an excellent command of the Chinese language that colleagues envied. She developed an obsession for honoring Chinese customs unless they were blatantly incompatible with Christianity.

Lottie also disciplined herself to survive physically and emotionally while living in primitive circumstances with the poorest of Chinese people. She learned to endure scrutiny and commentary by curious people who gave her no privacy.

Conquering fears of people who continually reviled her as "Devil Woman," she stayed courageous in the face of death threats, and she kept her poise with the Chinese military.

Lottie came to accept the "real drudgery" of mission life to experience God's presence in her life. She viewed her harsh realities by remembering that Chinese peasants were living a simple existence. An existence Jesus identified with.[36]

Perhaps, Lottie's deepest struggle was with loneliness. She wrote, "I hope no missionary will ever be as lonely as I have been." She battled with physical illness and depression much of her missionary life. [37]

Yet, despite her ailments, hope guided her. She wrote, "I would I had a thousand lives that I might give them to China!"[38]

Loneliness is an inevitability for many workers. It's unavoidable. How you deal with your loneliness can determine whether you finish your journey or list in waters of despondency.

As I read the biographies of great missionaries of the past, one constant rings true. Their hope sprang from the incarnate *logos*—Jesus Christ—and the written *biblos*—The Bible—which guided them towards their final shore.

Sail On

Okay. You read the Bible. Right? But—what guides you on your current journey? Is it God's Word or something else? What's the something else in your life?

_____

_____

_____

When confronted with ill will towards another, what's your response? When envy rears its ugly head, where do you turn? Do you respond in a way that honors God?

When discouraged, depressed, or despondent, who or what keeps you afloat? Helps to corrects your course? Leads you towards better waters of thought? Take some time. Write down your thoughts.

_____

_____

_____

_____

 True North

Your word is a lamp to guide my feet and a light for my path.

Psalm 119:105

Light House

The Bible points us towards our True North. Apart from it, our efforts are fraught with distress.

Have you smiled yet today?

Survival Tip #6

Pursue Personal Holiness

Follow peace with all men, and holiness, without which no man shall see the Lord:

Hebrews 12:14 KJV

Our old history ends with the Cross; our new history begins with the resurrection.

Watchman Nee, The Normal Christian Life

SAILS ARE FRAGILE, REQUIRING SPECIAL CARE. For example, flogging of the sails—sails flapping in the breeze—is the quickest way to allow sail degradation.[39]

Also, improper storing of sails, exposure to ultraviolet light, or failure to wash sails regularly will render a boat powerless to catch the winds energy. Tattered, dry, and rotted sails leave a boat helpless.

To me, those sails resemble holiness. Holiness safeguards a soul's integrity harnessing God's empowerment for life and service. When our soul is in excellent condition, we can catch the winds of the Holy Spirit described in Ephesians 5:18, "Be filled with the Spirit."

Often when I think about holiness, my mind goes back to the teachings— and enforcements—in my younger years that produced both confusion and anxiety about the matter.

The No-No's

Growing up in the Catholic Church, my understanding of holiness revolved around not committing certain sins. In Catholicism, you can commit a venial or mortal sin.

Venial sins got you in trouble; mortal sins sent you to hell. Apart from confession, penance, and absolution, a person stood in eternal damnation for perpetrating a mortal sin. As a young kid, mortal sins were not within my inclinations, but venial sins occurred a lot. Often, I entered the confessional to confess my sins to a priest fearing the loss of my soul.

The list of venial sins set before me during Confirmation classes threatened entrance into purgatory — a temporal place where one paid for their sins through immense suffering.

Talking back to your parents, stealing, grumbling, eating meat on Friday, going to unapproved movies, and considerable other little vices were sins to steer clear from. We called those sins The No-No's.

In 1973 when I got "saved" an additional set of prerequisites to holiness entered my vocabulary. The Baptist No-No's List marked hosts of other things to avoid in pursuit of holiness. It was exhausting trying to identify, remove, or stay away from all those no-no's.

No slacks on women, no cussing, no missing church, no long hair on men, and as Sonny and Cher used to sing, "The beat goes on." Oh, and no Sonny and Cher either. Began thinking those many years ago as a sixteen-year-old teen, "Wow! You have to give up a lot to be a Christian."

My son's father-and-law, who grew up in the Church of the Nazarene once commented as I shared this story, "Oh, yah, we had those too! We called them the Nazarene No-No's."

Their no-no's resembled verbatim most of the no-no's in our Baptist church. The biggest no-no most churches seemed to hold in common was, "Thou shalt not attend any other church, but our church." To attend another church was a no-no.

These no-no's also focused upon the social ills of the day. They went like this:

Thou shalt not drink.
Though shalt not smoke.
Thou shalt not dance.
Though shalt not be around people unlike us.
Thou shalt not go to movies. All movies are terrible.
Thou shalt not dress like this or that.

Thou shalt not listen to unchristian music. The Who, Eagles, Beatles, Creedence Clearwater Revival, AC/DC, and John Denver were all out. I soon learned the definition of Christian music. Christian music is whatever they liked, and I did not.

Thou shalt not, not, not, not...

One thing the No-no's seemed to accomplish efficiently was creating a smug group of self-righteousness people who defined holiness as abstinence.

What Holiness is Not

Holiness is not a list to follow, but rather a Person to pursue. That Person is Jesus Christ. When Jesus becomes the center of our holiness, rules cease as relationship grows, and behavior becomes more like Christ.

For example, the more I love my wife Kathy, the less need there is for a list of do's and don'ts. My desire to stay faithful to her goes far beyond, "Thou shalt not commit adultery."

> Holiness is not a list to follow, but rather a Person to pursue.

The more I love my sons and their families, my desire for them far exceeds, "Thou shalt not hurt your sons, nor their wives, nor their children."

See where I'm going with this?

Holiness in the Bible

Looking at the words "holiness" and "holy" in the Bible, themes emerge. When holiness occupied people, it produced a dedication singularly focused upon God.

For example, the items of the Temple in the Old Testament were holy. Meaning they were dedicated to pursuing God in worship and service. The more people pursued God; God became the most important Person in their lives.

Holy people mentioned in the Bible were God-people. They made much of God. God consumed their souls so that nothing else muzzled their worship.

Holiness directs us more towards God than to moral codes enforced by ecclesiastical influences. Personal holiness is the pursuit of Jesus Christ over the observance of church policies and rules.

73

The Apostle Paul talked about this very principle when writing a letter to a group of believers in the ancient city at Corinth in modern south-central Greece. He said,

> I want to know Christ and experience the mighty power that raised him from the dead.
>
> Philippians 3:10

That power that raised Christ from the dead is God. To know God's power, God's person, and God's presence, this is holiness.

Holiness then is a daily quest for closeness in relationship. When my pursuits focus upon the Father, there is little margin left to pursue unwholesome habits or activities.

Holiness in Christ

One day all people—past, present, and future—who are in Christ Jesus will stand before God. This event will mark a perfect holiness; a completeness.

Because of Christ, we can enter God's presence without a single flaw that might otherwise hinder our access to him. God views those in Christ as holy.

> Yet now he has reconciled you to himself through the death of Christ in his physical body. As a result, he has brought you into his own presence, and you are holy and blameless as you stand before him without a single fault.
>
> Colossians 1:22

Some refer to this as positional holiness. Holiness that atones—covers over—for our sin through Christ's work on the cross.

74

And not only so, but we also joy in God through our Lord Jesus Christ, by whom we have now received the atonement.

Romans 5:11 KJV

During my years in South Africa, one of our Zulu pastors said in English, *"We are holified in Jesus."* Though grammatically incorrect, he nailed it. We are holified—made holy—in Jesus Christ.

The challenge for believers is to live the holiness already granted to us in Christ.

Personal Holiness

There are many thoughts, actions, and activities that squelch holiness, and must be avoided. In today's hyper-grace movements, sin among believers is little addressed and even tolerated.

I've sat among Christians who allowed themselves many vices that the Scriptures denounce. Holiness wasn't part of their spiritual DNA because they misunderstood grace. Grace is not a permission for promiscuity, an excuse for weakness, but a path to catch God's Spirit directing us towards better waters of life and service.

An absence of holiness creates a void; a hole that looks for filling. We do not operate well in a vacuum of nothingness. Without holiness, all kinds of unhealthy thoughts bend us towards lust. Lust guides us to sin. And sin's finale leads to death. [40]

With an absence of holiness conflict fills our souls. Worry and anxiety blow us astray. Moral fragility weakens us. We drift from the very Person we claim to believe and trust in — Jesus.

You don't hear the word holiness much anymore. We've deemed it archaic, old fashioned. Perhaps that is one reason so much immorality exists among believers today.

75

Immorality leaves many Christians—including missionaries—without Godward momentum in their lives. While seeking to fill our sails with all kinds of concoctions of spirituality, one spiritual quality often lacks in our lives; holiness.

The Opposite of Holiness

It wasn't long ago someone informed me that a missionary abandoned his family in a remote place in a third-world country. The missionary boarded a plane leaving his wife and children to pursue another woman.

The incident was heartbreaking. Another broken marriage. Another damaged family. Children whose father tainted their perception of God. Scars that live on within the children of divorce. Fathers who act religious, but reject godliness.

This, unfortunately, is not a sole example within missionary ranks. Several other faces of missionary men come to mind who abandoned their families in a similar way. And not only men, women too. Missionaries from Charismatic to Baptist, orthodox to reform, who allowed unwholesome thoughts and activities to enter their souls, shipwrecked their lives upon the rocks of immorality.

The Scripture is clear:

But among you there must not be even a hint of sexual immorality, or of any kind of impurity, or of greed, because these are improper for God's holy people.

Ephesians 5:3

Jesus More, Jesus Most

For me, *holiness is Jesus more, Jesus most.* When my energies focus upon Christ, my soul's sails catch the Spirit blowing Christ's presence upon my life. If I set my course upon following Jesus more, following Jesus most, I become spiritually focused on treating others better, filtering my media viewing, offering forgiveness, and loving God.

Holiness guides my soul to steer clear of that which might tear its sails. When Jesus is more, and Jesus is most, the Spirit guides me to bridal my tongue rather than wounding another person with a verbal rashness that often falls from the lips. No other wind causes more damage than misspoken words oozing from an unholy heart.

The call to holiness is not a call to behave. [41] It's a call to belong. Paul instructed his young protégé Timothy to live holy.

For God saved us and called us to live a holy life. He did this, not because we deserved it, but because that was his plan from before the beginning of time—to show us his grace through Christ Jesus.

2 Timothy 1:9

Holiness is a belonging, a believing, a becoming. It's gravitating towards Jesus while staying away from anything that might detract me from him.

For me, holiness rests upon four words. *Jesus More, Jesus Most.* It's simple. It's direct. And it's effective. Most of all, it helps me make the most of Christ in my life.

Sail On

Jesus More, Jesus Most.

How might you make more of Jesus in your life?

_____

_____

_____

_____

_____

How can you make Jesus most?

_____

_____

_____

_____

 True North

Give unto the Lord the glory due to His name; Worship the Lord in the beauty of holiness.

Psalm 29:2 NKJV

78

We have been rescued from our enemies so we can serve God without fear, in holiness and righteousness for as long as we live.

Luke 1:74-75

Because we have these promises, dear friends, let us cleanse ourselves from everything that can defile our body or spirit. And let us work toward complete holiness because we fear God.

2 Corinthians 7:1

 Light House

Holiness is not a set of rules to follow but a Person to pursue. That Person is Jesus. Make Jesus more in your life. Make Jesus most in your life. For in this, holiness abandons a list of rules to follow, preferring to embrace the One who gave his life for us.

When your smiling, when your smiling, the whole world...

When Your Smiling by Louis Armstrong

Survival Guide # 7

Value Soul's Worth Above Self's Work

The first great and primary business to which I ought to attend every day is to have my soul happy in the Lord.

George Mueller

IN MARK 8 AND MATTHEW 16, Jesus admonished his disciples,

What do you benefit <u>if</u> you gain the entire world but *lose your own soul*?

Unfortunately, much of Evangelical Christianity relegates this verse to a momentary decision of salvation; to receive Christ. While it is true, upon receiving Christ–John 1:12 and Colossians 2:6–we gain eternal life, I don't think that's what Jesus was talking about here.

Looking closely at Jesus' words in its context, Jesus directed these words mostly towards Peter. Not an unbelieving Peter, but a Peter who endeavored to follow Christ. It's a far stretch of any interpretation to hold that Peter was not a believer here. Christ's statement was also more of a rebuke—warning—than a comforting assurance of eternal destination. Look:

> Then Jesus began to tell them that the Son of Man must suffer many terrible things and be rejected by the elders, the leading priests, and the teachers of religious law. He would be killed, but three days later he would rise from the dead.

> As he talked about this openly with his disciples, Peter took him aside and began to reprimand him for saying such things. Jesus turned around and looked at his disciples, then *reprimanded Peter*. "Get away from me, Satan!" he said. *'You are seeing things merely from a human point of view, not from God's.'*

> Then, calling the crowd to join his disciples, he said, *'If any of you wants to be my follower, you must give up your own way, take up your cross, and follow me.*

> If you try to hang on to your life, you will lose it. But if you *give up your life for my sake and for the sake of the Good News*, you will save it.

> And what do you benefit if you gain the whole world but lose your own soul? *Is anything worth more than your soul?'*

> Mark 8:31-36–Italics mine

81

Jesus asked a rhetorical question, "Is there anything more important than your soul?" The Greek language in which Jesus spoke indicates that Jesus plainly revealed his impending death. These words are also in the imperfect Greek tense showing that Jesus perhaps repeated them more than once.[42]

It's also probable that Peter physically pulled Jesus aside. Peter grabbed Jesus, and then reprimanded him.

Jesus' response was crushingly brutal, "Hey, Peter. Satan! Get behind me! You don't really care about what God wants. You only care about what you want."

Take hold of this for a moment. Let's put this into a modern-day Christian context. Peter was a top leader of the church. Authored many books, he'd been a sought-after speaker, or perhaps a celebrity pastor. Yet Jesus censured Peter's motives because Peter valued his work above his soul.

Jesus, "Peter, you don't care about my Father at all."
Peter, "Yes, Jesus, I really do care for you. Look at the things I'm doing for you!"
Jesus, "Peter, you are Beelzebub. You have no part in me. Get out of the way."

All this happened after Jesus had just finished saying, "You are blessed, Simon, son of John... And I will give you the keys of the Kingdom of Heaven. Whatever you forbid on earth will be forbidden in heaven, and whatever you permit on earth will be permitted in heaven."

Talk about messing with your mind! Peter must have thought, "What's up with all this?"

I think the narrative asks, "What does any of our god-pursuits matter if we lose our souls—lose ourselves—in quest of it?" It's a matter of focus, our actual intention, our worship.

I think Jesus questioned Peter's worship. Beyond our singing, music, and programming, Jesus asks, "What do you value most?" We value what we worship.

Our Worthship Dilemma

The word 'worship' finds its roots in an old English word 'worthship.' Our worship defines the worthship of what we value most.

Jesus valued his Father's will above all else. Every miracle he performed showed the worthship of his Father. Every word he spoke pointed towards what he valued most, God. To do his Father's will, above all else, was at the heart of Jesus' life.

> What we worship, we value.

Peter's plans didn't allow for a crucified Christ. He couldn't grasp that Jesus' ultimate act of worship would be to follow his Father's will to a horrible death on the cross, a death that provided the only remedy for sin.

Peter attempted to commandeer the moment, to make himself the object of the conversation. He forgot the many conversations and instructions of Jesus.

For I have come down from heaven to do the will of God who sent me, not to do my own will.

And this is the will of God, that I should not lose even one of all those he has given me, but that I should raise them up at the last day.

For it is my Father's will that all who see his Son and believe in him should have eternal life. I will raise them up at the last day.

John 6:38-40

We struggle with the same dilemma as Peter. We constantly remove God from the center of our worship, replacing God with something else.

The Object of Our Worship

Jesus clarified the essence of worship:

Then Jesus said to his disciples, 'If any of you want to be my follower, you must give up your own way, take up your cross, and follow me.'

Luke 9:23

Deny yourself, take up your cross, and follow me. These words pointed people to take up the scourge of the ancient era; a cross. The cross was a despised symbol of that day as it pointed to only one significance, suffering and death.

The message of Jesus' words was to want Christ more than self. To value God in my life above my own desires, plans, and ways of thinking.

Jesus asks, "Who is your Lord? Who's at the center of your thinking, Me or you?" It's an issue of worship.

Our soul finds significance in what we value most, what we find worthful. *What do we worship then? The God of our work, or the work of our God?*

George Mueller, the famous English evangelist and missionary who help found the Plymouth Brethren, and directed the Ashley Down orphanage in Bristol nails it here:

According to my judgement the most important point to be attended to is this: *above all things see to it that your souls are happy in the Lord.* Other things may press upon you, the Lord's work may even have urgent claims upon your attention, but I deliberately repeat, it is of supreme and paramount importance that you should seek above all things to have your souls truly happy in God Himself! Day by day seek to make this the most important business of your life. *The secret of all true effectual service is joy in God, having experimental acquaintance and fellowship with God Himself.*" Italics mine.

Somehow, we as Sent One's get more wrapped up in our work's inadequacies or competencies than Christ's sufficiency. It becomes a soul struggle as we fall into the trap of accomplishment over the adoration of our God.

Missionaries—perhaps like Peter—we do this all the time? Telling Jesus what's best for our plans, lives, and ministries? Charting out a course of service while we give only brief consideration of the Person for whom we're doing the work.

Prepare Your Soul

Unhealthy souls tend to drift towards unfavorable waters of busyness for God. The work of the church. The need of the poor. Demands of our denominations. Policies to follow. Finances to raise. Crushing challenges of missionary life. Yes, these things are important, but not at the cost of losing your soul—yourself—in all the pursuance.

Your soul is the vessel that carries you through all of life. If you lose yourself in all your missionary activities, what's the point?

I've seen missionaries lose themselves many times—I did.

In construction of their buildings.
In raising of their financial support.
In the branding of their ministries.
In the promotion of their causes.
In loneliness as they focused upon their aloneness.
In sin, while claiming to live for God.
In their successes.
In the murky waters of worry and anxiety.
In the overwhelming needs of the poor.
In…

It brings a thought...

Is it possible for us to lose ourselves in our work for God, leaving us dry, empty, and unfulfilled? I think so.

The exchange between Peter and Jesus suggests this possibility. Missionary lives can exist in a hollow dry place when we emphasize our soul's work over our soul's worth.

It's a matter of priorities. What takes the highest regard in your life? What do you hang onto above other consideration?

Hanging on to money–**my** support.
Hanging on to position–**my** ministry.
Hanging on to **my** expectation.
Hanging on to **my** structures.
Hanging on to projecting **my** best image.
Hanging onto **my** desires.
Hanging on to **my** expectations of missionary life.
Hanging on to **my** way of doing church.
Hanging on to...

The challenge for good soul-health is to deny yourself, take up your cross, and follow Christ daily. When God's worthship is central in our soul, good soul-work follows.

Deny Yourself

Denial of self focuses upon another life other than our own. To follow Jesus is to look away from our own identities, seeing self through Christ. For cross-cultural workers, the demands upon life and ministry require other denials too.

I posed another question to care providers and missionaries.

"What must missionaries learn to deny themselves to serve, survive, and thrive on their fields?"

Dozens of workers and care providers responded. Astounding was the regularity of which some responses occurred. Here are the top replies:

Deny your Cultural Values. Worker after worker cited this as a hard lesson learned. A missionary's culture is exactly that; the missionary's culture. The country and people a missionary serve know little about a Sent One's culture. Neither do they care.

A common cry heard from many seasoned cross-cultural workers was, "Learn to embrace the culture of the people you serve rather than expecting them to embrace yours."

Upon arriving in South Africa in 1986, we tried for several years to observe our Thanksgiving, 4th of July, Labor Day, Memorial Day, and our Christmas seasonal habits. In our third year, we gave up on most those observances.

My holidays meant nothing to South Africans, except for Easter and Christmas. But even with Christmas, our Zulu friends struggled to understand our emphasis of that holiday.

South Africans celebrate Easter far more than Christmas. To them, Easter was the day Jesus resurrected and was far more valuable than the commercialized Western Christmas season.

It constantly amazes me watching workers trying to inject their own politics, cultural values, and religious practices into the lives of the people they're trying to reach for Christ. Whose disciples are we making anyway, our own or followers of The Way? Acts 19:23

It would do cross-cultural workers well to put most of their cultural practices in the back seat of missionary work and embrace the culture of the people to whom they minister.

Deny your Exclusivity. Particularly relevant to first-world missionaries is an attitude of, "Our way is better than your way." This is true with many Western missionaries, especially Americans.

Many missionaries from other countries responded here. One Russian missionary commented, "When American missionaries arrive, they constantly bombard us with how much better their hospitals are compared to ours. They complain about our stores, food, traffic, weather, and… well, just about everything else. Who needs that?"

Upon entering South Africa, we moved into a middle-class white neighborhood in Ladysmith, South Africa. Under Apartheid Law, living among the Zulus was prohibited because of the color of our skin.

Observing other missionaries who arrived before us, I noticed that some bought expensive homes in exclusive areas with inground swimming pools, and luxury vehicles. Purposing to enter a more modest lifestyle, we moved into a middle-class neighborhood, purchased modest vehicles, and set ourselves apart from other missionaries by purchasing South African furnishings for our home rather than importing American items.

Even in this, many South Africans considered us wealthy—white and black—because of our origin of birth, the flights we took back and forth to the United States, and the dollars we brought into the country. No matter what we did, we were always the foreigner.

Yet missionaries in Europe, Australia, Japan, and other countries struggle to maintain even the most modest of lifestyles. With currency challenges, high expenses, and fluctuating support levels, it's difficult just to survive financially.

Here's a question I learned to ask myself.

"When people look at me, what do they see?"

That question may bend your noodle if you're honest with yourself.

Do people see Jesus in you, or do they see a forceful personality who has to be in charge?

Here's the thing, my friend. The "Mission Field" and its people don't need you or me. People need the Lord. Frankly, a sense of Christ's presence from Western missionaries is rare because of what they project; an image more about methodologies, persuasions, and opinions over the person of Jesus Christ.

You know what the national people think? A song that comes to mind is from MC Hammer's 90s song, *You Can't Touch This*. You probably think I'm a heathen now.

A young missionary's response put my mortality into view when he responded, "Who's MC Hammer?"

> Do people see Jesus in you, or a forceful personality who has to be in charge?

We become the Untouchables. They can't touch us, nor can we touch them with the truth of the gospel because they can't see Jesus through all the foam and mist spraying about in the density of our cultural exclusivities. We arrive and remain those who possess little in common among the people in which we live.

The late Daniel T. Niles, a famous Tamil pastor from Ceylon, Sri Lanka, proposed a fresh perspective.[43] He wrote,

> The missionary, he said, is a beggar telling other beggars where they would find bread. We are beggars, then, the difference being that we know where to go for food and the others don't.[44]

One of the greatest compliments I received in South Africa was when a Zulu friend introduced me to his neighbors.

He said, "Lona, umfundisi Mingo, yena umuntu ngumuntu ngabantu."

Meaning, "This is pastor Mingo. He is who he is because of how he relates and treats us."

Zulus say this when complimenting another black person. In that, he used this proverbial saying to pay me the highest honor ever given to me during my twenty-years in South Africa.

"This is pastor Mingo; he is a person like we are people."

Don't be exclusive. Try to bond with the people. Attempt to become one of them knowing that you'll never fully succeed, but it's a step towards the people, not away.

Deny your God-complex. Maggie—a missionary—responded, "Missionaries need to deny the compulsion to 'save' people and meet everyone's needs and do it perfectly."

You can't save everyone. You won't save everyone. Don't hoist that sail up your soul's mast.

I know. I was there too. But trying to help everyone was not the model of Jesus' life. He healed some, but many—the more—suffered on. Jesus fed the 3,000 and the 5,000, but that did not ease world hunger. He raised the dead, but they died again.

Jesus regularly said "no" to throngs of people who formed flotillas of desperation around him. He often separated himself from them. While offering himself to the entire world–John 3:16–he did not allow people to become the compass of his life and activity.

God created us in Christ to do good works. Ephesians 2:10 Jesus commanded us to let our lives shine so people may see our good works and look to God. Matthew 5:16

Our task then is to shine.

Shining relieves the pressure from me and grasps that the Holy Spirit draws people to God, not me. Yes, God works through us and in us, but that is to accomplish his purpose, not ours.

Remember the parable of the talents? The master gave one servant five talents, another two, and the last servant one talent. The servant with five talents doubled the master's holdings to ten. The next with two talents again doubled it to four. What did the master say to both servants?

"Well done. You've both been faithful."

We're sent into the harvest to serve. The size of the field and the harvest are up to God. Take a deep breath and exhale. Relax. Remove the pressure from yourself to carry the weight of the world. Jesus already did that.

Deny your Offendedness. In my years of service, two phrases come up often.

"They really hurt my feelings."
"They, them, he, or she offended me."

Surrounded by words or phrases like:

Betrayed
Disappointed
Unappreciated
Ignored
Taken for **granted**
They **used** me
They **forgot me**
They **abandoned** me
They **misunderstood** me
I am always **overlooked**

Jesus' words to his disciples are most instructive here:

Then he said to the disciples, 'Anyone who accepts your message is also accepting me. *And anyone who rejects you is rejecting me.* And anyone who rejects me is rejecting God, who sent me.'

Luke 10:16 Italics Mine

As a missionary, I promise that once you reach the field and spend a few years serving, you will fade into the background with relationships, supporters, and even—probably—your church.

This is the nature of human dynamics. The old saying, "Out of sight, out of mind," is too true here.

We should prepare for this eventuality. It is the price we must willingly pay to follow Christ.

Offendedness digs deep holes of bitterness; holes that will bury your soul. Offendedness is the stuff of many missionaries' grievances.

Missionaries don't get along. That is a fact. It's been true since the days of Hudson Taylor till now. Every missionary team I've ever observed—and, I mean, every—eventually disintegrated through offenses committed against another. Refusal to forgive and reconciled proves the biggest offense of all.

Paul and Barnabas erupted into a disagreement, and it fractured their relationship. It seems within our nature regardless of our calling as missionaries is the tendency to not get along. As we fight, dispute, and divide, we leave the people we're called to reach without Christ and without hope.

If we'd just obey the words of the one we claim to follow, my how different relationships might be.

"So now I am giving you a new commandment: **Love** each other. *Just as I have loved you*, *you should love each other*. Your love for one another will prove to the world that you are my disciples."

John 13:33-35 Emphasis Mine

But we don't obey, let alone love like Christ loved the Twelve. We don't show this world that we are his followers. Is it any wonder that so many reject a message we ourselves fail to live?

Deny your offended spirit. Take it on the chin. Ask yourself, am I paying attention to the reason I am offended? Curt Thompson MD puts it this way in his book, *The Anatomy of the Soul*, "How well am I paying attention to what I am paying attention to?" [45]

What's really at the center of your offense? Often, the offense, when examined, points towards a dearth or injury in our own lives.

If you love Jesus more, love him most, you will forgive and overlook an offense. King Solomon, the son of David, put it this way,

> Love prospers when a fault is forgiven, *but **dwelling on** it separates close friends.*

> Proverbs 17:9 Emphasis Mine

Deny your offendedness. It may be necessary to separate from another, but never let it be over your petty feelings.

Deny your Comparability. Sitting with a South Africa friend and missionary, he drew comparisons.

South African born, he married a young woman from Ireland. She, too, desired to serve as a missionary. They raised their support and worked among the Zulu people close to us. After ten years of working together, we became close friends.

Sitting together over coffee, Paul shared, "You know, Jackie and I realized how much farther ahead our friends are compared to us. This is true both with Jackie's friends in Ireland, and my friends here in South Africa."

Paul alluded to the plush homes, nice cars, and other fancies of life that their friends enjoyed, which they did not.

I responded, "Do they enjoy all those things, or do they just possess them?"

I could relate. I remember our first furlough. We served in South Africa six years before returning home. When I got there, wow! My friends had big new houses, nice cars, Ping Golf Clubs, and the list went on.

What really took me back were all the niceties their children enjoyed. Compared to the Old South African school my sons attended, those kids enjoyed the best schools, clubs, and activities. An overwhelming sense of *second-class citizen* came over me.

Sharing this with a friend of mine he retorted, "Don, yes, as a missionary, you'll give up much compared to your friends. But when compared to Jesus, you give up nothing."

His words were true. When compared to Christ, we give up nothing.

Take Up Your Cross

When we understand the cost and significance of the cross in our lives, it is there that we find Christ's inner peace and joy. In a daily acceptance of the cross, we find a deep sense of God's closeness to us.[46]

It is the cross that gives us peace and power over *pride* and *selfishness*. The two traits that are probably the most destructive of all imperfections. In embracing the cross daily, we show our love and obedience to follow Jesus.[47] No amount of service we perform pleases our Savior apart from the cross.

Any attempt at submitting to Christ begins with the cross. Only in a daily carrying of the cross do we see the full submission of Christ to the Father. His cross is our example of obedience. By the cross, he purchased freedom from the heavy weight of our sins.

Jesus told his disciples to, "... take up your cross and follow me." Beyond the example of Jesus carrying his own cross, we are never told exactly what the cross is; my cross, or your cross.

Perhaps the reason for this is that everyone's cross is different. The cross— or, crosses—I must carry may not resemble yours. Your obstacles to following Christ may differ from mine.

For one, it's an addiction. For another, it's apathetic spirituality. Fear hinders many from denying themselves to pursue Christ. Still others struggle with various lusts of the flesh and a list of impediments that might exceed the pages of this guide.

In addition, the missionary's cross differs because of the diverse lifestyles and challenges we encounter while trying to fulfill our callings. Here are some crosses we often carry.

Carry your Cross of Loneliness. Many workers continually cite loneliness as an experience and test of missionary life. In all the Scriptures read over the years, the counsel received, and the prayers uttered, I've come to believe that loneliness is a cross we must willingly carry rather than seeking to escape its presence.

If you're going to be a missionary, you're going to get lonely.

Kathy and I talk about his often. We have many who love us, who care for us, and respect us. But there is no one that is close to us.

Perhaps this is because of the many transitions and traveling we've done over the years. While we are thankful for those who love us, we often sit on our porch with a sense of loneliness. A feeling we quickly shake off.

To me, loneliness is part of the worker's calling. Accept it and see the positives of your aloneness.

In aloneness, we are never alone. God becomes close to us as we draw close to him. James 4:8

In aloneness, understand that Christ fully identifies and understands. Hebrews 4:15

In aloneness, realize that God will at some point extravagantly reward!

In loneliness, we better understand the cross our Savior gave himself to on our behalf. As he hung, tormented by the Romans, abandoned by his disciples, and railed upon by the crowd, loneliness assaulted Christ.

Isaiah wrote:

> "He was despised and rejected—
> a man of sorrows, acquainted with deepest grief.

We turned our backs on him and looked the other way.
He was despised, and we did not care."

Isaiah 53:3

Loneliness is a cross that can bring us closer to Christ. Lonesomeness helps us identify with Christ. It can make our journey with Christ become meaningful as we feel what Jesus felt. Loneliness need not push away from God. By seeing Christ in our aloneness, that empty space within our souls can experience God's presence, filling a gloomy disposition with hope.

Carry your Cross of Detachment. For me, one of the biggest challenges to missionary life was the sense of detachment from family, friends, and fellowships.

With much fanfare and hubbub, our church sent us off to South Africa. Four weeks later, we sat in an empty house, and in a neighborhood where we knew no one.

I'll never forget the sense of detachment.

Upon returning home six years later, family and friends changed as people got on with their lives during our absence. Any sense of belonging faded.

Then our sons began returning to the country of their births, went to college, got married, and settled down, seeking to *rarely move again.*

A sense of detachment overwhelmed us once again. I concluded that we must carry this cross, or spend our lives chasing after people to fill a need they can't possibly meet.

That's not to say that we don't enjoy a wonderful relationship with our sons and their families. However, we understand that we can't be present for every family event. Especially since our sons live thousands of miles apart. Besides, with 15 grandchildren, how could we ever make all the gymnastics tournaments, concerts, and other events?

I call each one of my grandchildren regularly, asking them about their hobbies, school, and interests. In all of this, Jesus' promise often comes to mind:

And everyone who has *given up* houses or brothers or sisters or father or mother or children or property, for my sake, *will receive a hundred times as much in return* and will *inherit eternal life.*

Mathew 19:29 Italics Mine

Jesus' words here offer comfort particularly for older missionaries who've spent their entire lives on their fields sacrificing what many take for granted.

Carry your Cross of Financial Instability. Many, if not most missionaries, struggle for lack of adequate resources. Many workers mentioned financial instability as a cross to carry. Several missionary women listed,

- Not having enough support to save for retirement.
- Not having the money to provide a permanent base on home assignment.
- We always have to stay in homes with other people.
- Even if you have the money to maintain two households—one house stateside and the other on the field—people will judge that you have too much money.
- Not being able to accept family heirlooms because you can't afford a house big enough to keep them, or pay for storage.
- Financial instability caused by loss of supporters and fluctuating exchange rates.
- Not being able to help your children the way your friends provide for theirs back home.

Enough said? Missionary women often mentioned financial insecurity as an impediment to missionary life, while men cited the lack of resources to conduct ministry efficiently.

Either way, you'll probably lack the funding you need to do what you want to do. In this, we must take up our cross.

Carry our Cross of Humility. Jesus' words speak to humility's entirety,

But among you it will be different. Those who are the greatest among you should *take the lowest rank,* and the *leader should be like a servant. Who is more important, the one who sits at the table or the one who serves?* The one who sits at the table, of course. But not here! *For I am among you as one who serves.*

Luke 22:26-27 Emphasis Mine

Carry our Cross of Suffering. Just this morning while working on this chapter, a missionary inbox me asking, "Hey Don, I've been asked to make a manual for missionaries who are planning to go to the field. Any suggestions?"

I immediately shot back:

To me, the biggest issue is, are you willing to die? Missionaries, particularly US missionaries, sail off to their fields too starry-eyed about missions.

They aren't prepared to suffer because no one has prepared them to endure hardships the field will bring. That's why so many quit at the first sign of trouble.

More and more, missionaries experience assaults, hijacking, burglaries, defrauds, and worse.

They need to understand this. They must count the cost before they go.

When James Calvert–19th Century British Missionary–went out to the cannibals of the Fiji Islands, the ship's captain tried to turn him back, saying, "You will lose your life and the lives of those with you if you go among such savages."

To that, Calvert replied, *"We died before we came here."*[48]

A more contemporary example is that of John Chau. In November 2018, an isolated tribe which he attempted to share Christ, killed him on Sentinel Island—an obscure island in the Indian Ocean.

Shortly after arriving on the island, the Sentinelese shot arrows at him. He paddled his kayak away from danger.

He wrote in his journal after being attacked by the islanders, "You guys might think I'm crazy in all this, but I think it's worth it to declare Jesus to these people."

His friends wrote of him, "I don't think any of us modern Western missionaries actually expect to die doing the work God has called us to. Yet John Chau was absolutely ready for that."[49]

Jesus put it this way,

> But don't begin until you count the cost. For who would begin construction of a building without first calculating the cost to see if there is enough money to finish it?
>
> Otherwise, you might complete only the foundation before running out of money, and then everyone would laugh at you.
>
> They would say, 'There's the person who started that building and couldn't afford to finish it!'
>
> Or what king would go to war against another king without first sitting down with his counselors to discuss whether his army of 10,000 could defeat the 20,000 soldiers marching against him?
>
> And if he can't, he will send a delegation to discuss terms of peace while the enemy is still far away.
>
> So you cannot become my disciple without giving up everything you own.
>
> Luke 14:25-33

Your soul's value is far above that of your work; what you do. Learn to value the health of your soul.

99

Sail On

Take a piece of paper, or maybe open your journal. Or perhaps on your computer, create a new file. Divide the page into two columns. On the top of one column write, *My Soul-works*. Over to the next column, write *My Soul's Worth*.

Ask yourself, "How does your work figure into your soul's priorities? Where are you following Jesus? How is your worship affected by your work?"

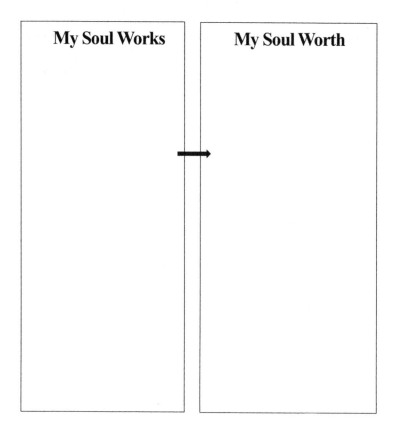

My Soul Works	My Soul Worth

True North

By the grace God has given me, I laid a foundation as a wise builder, and someone else is building on it. But each one should build with care.

For no one can lay any foundation other than the one already laid, which is Jesus Christ.

I Corinthians 3:10-11 NIV

For you died to this life, and your real life is hidden with Christ in God.

Colossians 3:3

 Light House

Make Jesus the center of your life and work. Refuse to lose yourself in the demands and busyness of ministry. Denying yourself is part of this process. Remember, Christ died for you, and your life—the real you—is hidden with Christ in God. This cross we must pick up and carry.

Smile though your heart is aching...Light up your face with gladness...

Smile by Nat King Cole

Survival Tip #8

Recognize Endings Reveal More Than Beginnings

It is not the going out of port, but the coming in, that determines the success of a voyage.

Henry Ward Beecher

...let us strip off every weight that slows us down, especially the sin that so easily trips us up. And let us run with endurance the race God has set before us.

Hebrews 12:1

LOOKING AT JEFF'S CATAMARAN SITTING in the harbor at Durban Point South Africa, the ocean sparkled in the calm waters of the waterfront.

We prepared for a journey of several days out in the open waters of the Indian Ocean to Mozambique. The weather forecast was favorable, and the crew was ready as we cast off.

Only a few hours into our voyage, seemingly out of nowhere, a storm came upon us. Well, a little squall really. The storm lasting only a few hours ushered me into the reality of sailing.

That pristine picturesque harbor in Durban quickly changed into a nightmare as Jeff, standing at the helm with both hands on the ship's wheel, smiled at my plight. With the waves pounding upon the catamaran, seasickness stripped me of any strength to assist the crew. As I repeatedly puked on the deck, the crew skillfully attended to the vessel.

Doubt screamed in my head, "What in the world are you doing out here! *What made you ever think you could ever…?*"

After the storm, in tranquil waters, Jeff chuckled.

"Don, we were never in any danger. My vessel is in good repair; the crew well trained. I know these waters well. That's the difference between enjoying the ocean or becoming another casualty, understanding the journey."

Jeff cleared his throat, and added, "*Going out of port is not as important as returning to port. If you get lost out there, what does any of your goings out matter? Endings reveal more than beginnings.*"

Jeff's comment stabbed my soul. I thought, "Ah… if we as missionaries could learn this? Endings reveal more than our beginnings."

🗺 The Lost Missionary

During my many years in South Africa, I often frequented Wimpy's. Seemed like every town in South Africa sported a Wimpy's in those days. It was a hamburger joint that was so much more than just a fast food establishment.

There you enjoyed table service, and food served on glass plates with real cutlery. Why plates and silverware for hamburgers and French fries? That is the unique nature of life in much of South Africa, and at Wimpy's. Many South Africans eat their burger and chips—french fries—with a knife and fork. It's considered appropriate for dinning.

Proper eating requires a knife and fork. The knife is used to pile food upon the back of an inverted folk, even for a hamburger. In this manner, dinning becomes more of a cultural event rather than just serving a basic need for a quick bite.

Our favorite reason for visiting was their coffee. Many mornings took place at Wimpy's over a beautiful cup of hot steaming coffee with whipped hot milk and a shovel full of sugar.

Wimpy's is where I met for the first time an old Swedish Baptist missionary. Let's call him Viggo. Our meeting occurred in the early 1990s. I was in my middle 30s as Viggo approached his 80th birthday. At the encouragement of his son, he agreed to meet with me. The object of the visit was for the senior missionary to encourage the younger. That meeting proved anything but encouraging.

Our talk proceeded nicely as I shared my vision for the surrounding areas of Ladysmith, South Africa. What started out as a casual conversation turned into a thought-provoking tragedy.

As he sipped his coffee he whimpered, "Don't waste your life here. I squandered mine. I've worked relentlessly, but have nothing to show for it. *I'm totally finished!*"

The phrase '*totally finished*' is a common expression used among English speakers in South African. It expresses, "At one's end, completely worn out, or in a hopeless state."

The elderly gentleman arrived in South Africa in the early 1950s, speaking only Swedish. He learned to master English, Zulu, and Afrikaans. An incredible feat as I struggled to learn Zulu.

Idolizing his language accomplishments, the conversation continued. From his deep wrinkled face, his cloudy blue eyes peered into my soul. With a sigh, he mumbled, "I've wasted my life with these people."

"What were you hoping to accomplish?" I asked.

His list included many admirable ambitions and goals. Far beyond anything I'd hope to see in my ministry. He gained much in ministry, much among his peers, much in his denomination, and much in his accomplishments. Yet, none of that satisfied him. While doing all the churchy stuff, the crescendo of his words continued to jolt. He looked down.

"I came here to save souls, but I think I lost mine."

🗺 Going It Alone Missionaries

Traveling extensively, visiting, and speaking to hundreds of missionaries, I often note that many fly solo in their endeavors. They live and serve, isolating themselves from other colleagues, their mission agency, and supporters.

This is not a problem, until there's a problem, and then it's a problem.

When an illness, death, mental health crisis, or need for Evac in a hostile situation arises, cross-cultural workers out there on their own, well… are out there alone. I can't tell you how many independent missionaries we've run across who made a courageous step to go to the field with no one behind them to hold the ropes.

Here's a stark truth about bearing one another's burdens. *You can't bear another's burdens if there's no one to bear your burdens.* Many missionaries lack burden bearers because they isolate themselves.

Jeff's words came to mind again when talking about his many voyages on the high seas. He once told me, "When a person gets in real trouble out here— the ocean—it's because they decided they don't need anyone's help. Anyone can take a quick cruise in the harbor, but it's a fool that heads out to deep waters alone. Many who head into open waters alone never return."

Missionary service is rarely a solo journey. While serving the many in our ministries, we can drain out while giving out leading to burning out. The biblical model is one another. Not one to the others. Paul nails this in 1 Thessalonians 3:12, "And may the Lord make…

105

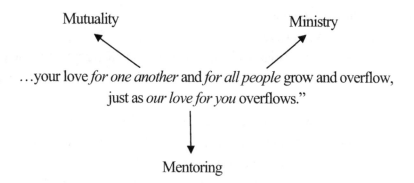

🗺 Use-To-Be Missionaries

After finishing our second Sunday morning service, I stood at the main entrance offering goodbyes. A couple approached me.

They visited our church way up in Northern Minnesota for the first time. They thanked me for the sermon. As they stepped through the door into the frigid Minnesota winter, he parted with, "Pastor Don, we used to be missionaries too."

This encounter stood out. Their demeanor. The look in their eyes. The emptiness in their smiles. Sitting at home that evening, their last words echoed, "We used to be missionaries too."

Seemed no one else knew they used to be missionaries. Then one day, while ordering my triple shot espresso extra hot toffee nut latte, there they stood behind me waiting for their order. Latte in hand, I asked to join them at their table.

Brian and Martha served as missionaries in Togo, Africa. Their ministry of church planting, feeding centers, and establishing a Bible Institute spanned 15 years. Fluent in French and Kabiyé, they revealed an amazing life and work. Now, they sat in front of me with aimless misdirection.

"We planned on staying in Togo our whole lives, but…" Brain stopped and looked down at the floor.

I asked, "But what Brian?"

For the next hour, Brian and Martha shared one hardship after another. Setbacks, disappointments, betrayals, drain outs, and then burnout. Sicknesses, transitions, and the coming and goings of new missionaries, each upon their arrival with a better way for conducting Brian and Martha's ministry.

"They never stayed long," Martha uttered, "Just long enough to point out the weaknesses and faults of our lives and works."

Their sending agency was unresponsive to their needs. Conflict among other personale in Togo surfaced too. Betrayals by some national leaders. Loss of financial support. The transitions of missionary life. One issue stood out above all others.

Martha spoke up, "And… every time we came back home, no one really cared."

I replied, "Cared…?"

"Yah, you know. When we came back. Supporters were too busy to spend time with us. They didn't care. With another new pastor at our Sending Church, our church was more foreign to us than Togo."

Brian and Martha told of five burglaries at their home. Added to that was a hijacking and two robberies.

Brian added, "You think anyone cared a thing about us when we talked of all this? Nope. They don't care. Way to busy to listen to our story. We've given up on the church. They used us."

Martha explained that to her missionary life was more about recruiting then caring.

She grumbled, "They told us it was an exciting venture; the missionary life. Visiting churches as newbie missionaries, we were young and energetic. Churches and people showed interest, but 10 years out they couldn't have cared less."

The kicker for Brian and Martha occurred when their field team made up of missionaries from their agency—most with less than five years' experience—voted against their dream of starting a second Bible Institute for the Kposo people.

On the day of the vote, two missionaries—relatively new to the field—voted against the idea.

Brian exhaled, "As the senior missionaries in Togo, a bunch of rookies who didn't even speak the language yet, ended our vision to move forward. That ended our desire to stay in Togo."

Their visit to our church in Northern Minnesota that Sunday morning was their first visit to church in five years. What happened?

Here's the tragic part of my encounter with Brian and Martha that day in a coffee shop on a frigid January morning. Brain and Martha dropped out. Dropped out of church. Dropped out of community. Dropped out of faith and dropped out with God.

Disappointment turned to anger. Anger accused of betrayal. Betrayal provided rich soil for bitterness to grow, corrupting their view of people, the Church and God.

Brian and Martha became unintentional agnostics. They still claimed to believe in God. It was… just that… God didn't seem to believe in them. To them God was unknowable, distant, and uncaring. Fact was, that they—not God—became distant and uncaring for God.

Martha kindly rejected my offer to pray with them. Martha's parting words pierced, "Don, we just don't have any use for that which used us up and threw us away."

On the drive home through the icy roads, I thought, "What did Brian and Martha anchor their soul to that allowed them to drift so far from a faith they once claimed to believe? A faith they proclaimed, but now loathed."

🗺 Hermit Missionaries

Katie served as a single missionary for over thirty years when we met her. As we spent time with her, an interesting trait surfaced. Katie was a hermit missionary.

Somewhere during her years of service, Katie dropped out. She still lived on the field, and collected her meager support every month. She rarely attended church services, and no longer took part in ministry unless supporters visited her field.

Katie's story of missionary life as a single woman was filled with distress. In tears she shared her story.

"I'm tired of trying to fit into a world of missionary couples. It's like a single missionary's only purpose is that of a nanny or schoolteacher."

Katie explained that anytime she formed a relationship with a guy in the country, her host missionaries—a married couple—worried she'd get into trouble.

"That happened once here when another female missionary got pregnant. Now, if I talk to any guy, my purity is suspected."

Katie admitted, "I know I'm just hiding out, but I've watched a dozen married missionary couples come and go over the years. Whenever a new couple arrives, I'm immediately under their supervision. I'm sick of it. I just outlast them, and usually they're gone within a few years."

She added, "My supporters have forgotten about me. As long as I'm on the field their ok with me. I live like a retired person."

Katie's not alone. Missionaries, after trying everything, often become field-side recluses. Missionaries on the field who are no longer in the field.

🗺 Refugee Missionaries

Sitting in my office in Northern Minnesota, my administrative assistant informed me of a phone call. Exhaling—showing my disproval of being disturbed—she insisted, "Pastor, sorry to bother you, but I think you need to take this call right now." Grudgingly I picked up the phone and answered, "Hello, this is pastor Don."

A sobbing missionary began, "Hello, this is R_____ M_____. Your church supports us. I'm sorry to inform you that we can't return to the Ukraine. We are in Iowa right now. We won't be able to return to the field."

A further conversation revealed his missionary wife suffered from severe Agoraphobia. This fear can be so overwhelming that one feels unable to leave their home.[50] This missionary wife after receiving a year of treatment, was still unable to leave their rented house in Iowa.

Some spiritual leaders surrounding them talked of her affliction as a result of "spiritual warfare" a "lack of faith" or a "failure of obedience."

The biblical counselors at their church concluded the missionary wife's problem was some hidden sin she refused to acknowledge; a failure to trust God fully.

Without compensation, care, or preparation, the mission's agency ended their missionary employment. The missionary—a MK—lost the only life he'd ever known.

R_____ shared with me, "It's like I'm a refugee here in Iowa. I hate it, but I don't know what else to do."

After listening for over an hour, I offered kind words.

"R_____, thank you for your faithful years of service. Thanks for putting the needs of your wife above your desire for ministry and missionary work.

Don't allow the title of missionary define who you are in Jesus Christ. You and your wife are children of God. Beloved in every way.

Find someone who can help your wife. A specialist with skills of dealing with house bound maladies. Believe it or not, your wife is not the only agoraphobic I know of in the missionary ranks.

I know God is faithful. May he show you his purpose in all of this. You're not a failure. You are my hero. God will right this one day."

With that, we sent this abandoned missionary couple a gift to help them through their financial difficulties.

🗺 3 Strikes and You're Out Missionary

In baseball, we call a batter standing at the plate out after swinging for the third time, and not making contacting with the ball. As a kid growing up playing baseball, many times I heard the umpire's call, "STRIKE THREE! YOUR OUT!" Of course, not for me, but—you know—for all the other players striking out.

One of the greatest tragedies I've witness among missionaries is what I identify as the *Three Strikes and You're Out Missionary.*

I'm not talking about when a missionary resigns and comes off the field. "Resigned" is a harsh word for simply changing ecclesiastical vocations. Christian workers change ministry, focus and jobs all the time. When a missionary decides to return from the field, the label "resigned" is often attached; a thoughtless misfortune.

What I'm speaking of comes from the words of a missionary spoken to me several years ago. Words—unfortunately—repeated by other missionaries, too.

That missionary looked me straight in the eyes and said, "I'm done. *Done* with ministry. *Done* with the Church. *Done* with God." Three strikes; done, done, and done.

THREE STRIKES AND YOUR OUT is a rare occurrence; no, it's not. Tracking down several missionaries after they returned from their fields found more than just a few shipwrecked in feelings, family, and faith.

Quickly forgotten by their sending organizations, churches and supporters, these missionaries drifted out of sight. While holding their own in life and ministry, they vanished in the depths of service.

Worse of all, such casualties often questioned the very Captain of their souls. Believing Jesus was their Rock, they held their own as faith's ship ran aground, abandoning what they once believed.

🗺 Traumatized Missionaries

Trauma is perhaps the most under discussed facet of missionary work. Assault, rape, robbery, physical injury, or exposure to death and despair affects the brain; even missionary brains.

We talk little about this magnificent organ God created. The brain and its amazing complexities are often something we throw a Bible verse at to those struggling with mental health issues.

The wear and tear of serving—especially in third world countries—punishes the mind, body, and soul. Christian missions often ignore the evitable consequences of such rigors of missionary life.

In my book *To Hell Back and Beyond—A PTSD Journey: When Faith and Trauma Collide,* I share the debilitating effects of my continue exposure to trauma, murder, and infant mortalities while serving among the Zulu people in South Africa.

Added to that were my childhood bruises, dislocated knuckles, welt marks on my skin from beatings with extension cords—the list could go on—from my childhood.

That all surfaced in my 40s in South Africa. The voyage—that affects both physical and mental health—caught me unaware. I discovered that I'm not unique here in my missionary experience.

Returning to the United States, I sought to pastor. Under the incredible stress and pace, plus the pressures of the American pastorate, my condition deteriorated.

After the insistence and offering of a pastor friend to pay to get me help, I began seeing Tom. Tom specialized in trauma. Within eight sessions, Tom diagnosed me with a moderate case of PTSD—Post Traumatic Stress Disorder. That diagnosis was confirmed by two other specialists over a ten-year period.

This malady once thought an affliction of only frontline soldiers almost destroyed my life. A medic friend who served in the war zones of Afghanistan and Iraq shared, "Don, you've seen as much as many soldiers today."

It's from this perspective I wrote *To Hell, Back, and Beyond*, hoping you'll not become the next missionary casualty who cannot recognize the warning signs of post-traumatic stress.

Listen, terrible things happen to missionaries. Our calling puts us at high risk of trauma. My guess—and it's only a guess—is that 1 out of 5 missionaries who've experienced traumatic events suffer long-term effects.

You must learn to deal with your trauma, or your trauma will deal with you.

My concern is for the large numbers of missionaries who once leaving the field isolate themselves—a very common trait of trauma—dropping out of community altogether. They end up buried in missionary service unhonored, unwept, and unsung.[51]

📖 Seaworthy Missionaries

Seaworthy is a term used to describe a vessel or person who is fit for sailing. The word does not imply that one person is less than another, but rather is a person fully prepared.

Recently, I attended a missionary reunion sponsored by our missionary sending agency. Over a hundred missionaries attended. All sorts of missionaries. Young and old. Married and single. Newbies, rookies, and seasoned workers.

Our director asked a question during the men's breakout session.

"What is one special thing about missionary life that's made it all worthwhile?"

In that room, sat battled seasoned missionaries who stayed their courses through the stormiest of voyages. One elder missionary raised his hand. His answer made—for me—the entire week a worthwhile investment of my time.

He said, "What's made it all worthwhile is keeping my eyes on the One who called me into the greatest life I could have ever lived; the missionary life."

Noteworthy was the amount of personal loss that graceful old missionary experienced over his life. Loss of his wife. Death of a child. Decline of his income when he advanced into aging years as churches discontinued his support. Burglarized more than a few times, robbed, and attacked too. Added this was his failing health as he entered his final years.

Yet, here a godly warrior righted my soul with his last words that morning.

"If you keep your eyes on Jesus, you can go through anything and not lose your hope. Your calling. Your reason for living and serving."

Wow… I want to be that kind of missionary.

Servanthood requires faithfulness. Sticking it out when things get tough. That doesn't mean you'll always remain on the "mission field," but it does mean we stay faithful to the One who began a good work in us. "And I am certain that God, who began the good work within you, will continue his work until it is finally finished on the day when Christ Jesus returns." Philippians 1:6

 Sail On

What type of missionary are you? What is the compass that guides you through your missionary calling, life, and service?

True North

"A faithful, sensible servant is one to whom the master can give the responsibility of managing his other household servants and feeding them. If the master returns and finds that the servant has done a good job, there will be a reward."

Matthew 24:45-46

"Keep your lives free from the love of money and be content with what you have, because God has said, 'Never will I leave you; never will I forsake you.'"

Hebrews 13:5 NIV

 Light House

Our beginnings means little if we fail to finish our course.

> Sail on,
> When the water gets high
> Sail on,
> When the wind starts to die
> It's just a matter of minutes
> Till His ship comes to get us
> And we'll all get in it
> — Sail On by The Imperials

And, what about that smile? Come on. You can do it.

115

Survival Tip #9

Secure Adequate Provisions

UNFORTUNATELY, MANY MISSIONARIES WHO LEAVE for their fields full of vision and passion arrive poorly financed. Tiring of fundraising and filled with anticipation, they cripple their ministries from the start, failing to provide adequately for their families, ministries, and themselves because of lack of capital.

Their reasons go something like this:

"We're going to just trust God and go!"

"After all, those promises for support will come once we arrive on the field."

"People need the Gospel more than I need to raise money."

"I'll come back in a few years and raise more support."

"God will supply."

Fiscal constraints are not the only reason for financial struggles. During our years in South Africa, we watched many fully funded missionaries struggle because of Draconian financial policies of their mission organizations. Economic survivability became impossible.

There are three groups of missionaries when it comes to finances. Those who lack, those who barely have enough, and those who enjoy full support.

Under Supported
- Often needs of the field exceeds the needs of family
- Limited resources for ministry
- Zero funds for emergencies, retirement, etc.

Adequately Supported
- Funds for adequate housing and family needs
- Some resources for ministry
- Little funds for emergency, travel, or retirement

Fully Supported
- Housing, children's schooling, and extras doable
- Fully resourced for ministry
- Emergency fund and retirement contributions possible

Don't Go Until...

Please listen, if you can't adequately care for your family's needs on the field, what business do you have going in the first place? The Apostle Paul told the young Timothy that anyone who didn't provide for their family had denied the faith and was worse than an unbeliever. 1 Timothy 5:8

Think about it. You're out there on the field doing Gospel work, but denying the very faith you proclaim because of domestic negligence. I see this all the time.

"God called me," you might say.

Ok then, did God's calling include neglecting the needs of your spouse and children? Now, please listen to me here.

Regularly as we travel, we meet missionaries living in countries with less than $1500.00 a month support; for a family of six! A missionary couple without funds to care adequately for their children, medical needs, or travel is one of the most heartbreaking things to witness. Living in awful accommodations for God is admirable, but I doubt your adult children, looking back upon their childhood years, will agree.

Is it any wonder that some TCK's—third culture kids—upon reaching adulthood, forsake the church, having nothing to do with it ever again? As one TCK told me, "The ministry got everything. We got nothing."

Prodigal MK or Prodigal Parents?

When I was in high school, I worked in the Housekeeping Department at Abbott Northwestern Hospital in Minneapolis, Minnesota. It was there I met Darrel during our lunch breaks.

Found out that Darrel was a missionary kid whose parents served in Asia for decades. He spoke Mandarin fluently. In his middle 20s, he was trying to get his footing back 'home' in Minnesota, a place in which he felt little acquainted.

Once during a lunch break, I spoke of my intention of becoming a missionary. His head snapped around as his demeanor became combative. His next words were sobering:

Don't get married and have kids then. It's not fair to make your kids go through all that. To watch your parents beg for money while never getting enough. Then come back here and see all the great stuff everyone else's kids have while I got nothing!

Not me. I'm done with the church. And, if that's how God works, I'm done with him too.

Ouch! Sigh… Cry…

Single missionaries also arrive on the field so under-supported that they struggle from the start. Their challenges and frustrations adjusting to life in an unfamiliar country while suffering from lack of backing can overwhelm.

Take the extra time to raise the support you need. If you can't raise enough support to care for yourself or family, ask yourself if there's another way to gain the necessary support?

Support-Rich but Cash-Poor

Once, while in South Africa, we met a single missionary from Australia. She worked at the local Emmaus Clinic in the mountains outside of Winterton, South Africa.

She possessed less than $500.00 a month support. That didn't matter because God provided through his people in many other ways.

A Christian family provided the house she lived in, she paid no rent, and local churches provided her with a small pickup truck!

During her many long hours at the clinic caring for the most destitute women and children, she often ate meals at the canteen which Emmaus hospital provided for their nurses.

Afrikaner farmers donated clothing. They also blessed her with gifts at Christmas and during her birthday. While she lacked liquidity, she enjoyed a high level of support.

God has many ways to provide for our needs as we serve him in the harvest fields of this world. I like Philippians 4:19:

> *But my God shall **supply all your need** according to his riches in glory by Christ Jesus.*

"Support" can take a variety of forms. While encouraging you to raise the funds you need, I also urge you to look to God foremost to provide for your needs.

Prepare for the Unexpected

Kathy and I traveled to her hometown in El Dorado, Kansas, twenty years ago. While there, we met a missionary widow. Still young—in her late 40s—she shared her demise. That is the exact word she used, "demise."

Her husband died after falling into a ravine while jogging in the country they served. Within a year after her husband's death, their supporters abandoned her. With little life insurance, she not only grieved the loss of her husband but suffered the added indignity of lacking an adequate income.

With little provision, she lived in a derelict trailer in a rundown mobile home park. She suffered from loneliness, depression, and lack of companionship.

A simple life insurance policy, cheap enough when your young, could have changed the trajectory of her life after the death of her husband. Instead, her soul listed under the weight of her trials. Overwhelmed, her faith sunk under waves of doubt and despair.

When You Get Old

You'll probably get old someday. Many elderly missionaries struggle just to get by. Upon returning home, they often lack necessities; housing, retirement, or income.

I just spoke with a couple today who spent thirty-five years serving overseas. Now—in their 70s—they both work full-time jobs, are in poor health and had to purchase their furniture on credit.

While in Bible college, my pastor encouraged us to "just trust God!" He didn't believe in saving for retirement. To him, that showed a lack of faith. He was my friend, and I respected him.

When he got older—hindered by health problems—his younger wife supported him, working fifty-hour workweeks. He died, leaving her penniless, unable to support herself any longer in her declining health.

Find some way to save for retirement because once you've outlived your productiveness on the field, most of your churches and supporters will slowly discontinue your support. This is the Law of Attrition.

While the Law of Attrition applies to a declining workforce, it also includes "the act of wearing or grinding down by friction."[52] I think this definition applies to long-term missionary work.

Once, an associate director of a large missions agency made a comment from the platform during a World Missions Conference. He chided the missionaries present by saying, "I don't know what it is about missionaries, but once they reach fifty-five years of age, they just sort of sit down, sort of retire."

In my younger days, I was not near as diplomatic as I've learned to be today. Approaching him after the service, I said, "I know the answer about those sit-down missionaries."

He replied, "What? What answer?"

I shot back, "Why they sit down at fifty-five."

"Why then," he frowned back at my aggressive approach.

"Well, the reason they just sit down or retire is that serving and living on the field grinds the life out of you. They are not lazy; they're worn out."

As you get older, so do your supporters. Some die. Others retire, readjusting their lives to their own retirement incomes. And others drop off the radar of your ministry.

When you hit your 70s, the leaders of your supporting churches will probably be in their 40s. That's a thirty-year gap between at least two generations.

A young pastor recently shared—more like told me—"I'm not supporting old missionaries who can't work anymore. It's their fault they didn't put adequate money aside for their retirement. That's not my problem. Besides, there are younger missionaries begging for support."

That young pastor—thirty years my junior—had zero concept of what it was like for a missionary in the 70s, 80s, and 90s to save for retirement. Neither did he care.

Upon our approval for missionary service in 1984, a well-meaning veteran missionary influencer in our group spoke to several of us—young missionaries—about retirement.

Our options were limited in those days. The internet virtually didn't exist. No smart phones either. No online investing with Vanguard, Merrill Lynch, TD Ameritrade, or the like.

And few—if any missionaries—enjoyed pensions, 401k's, or other retirement vehicles.

Our older missionary friend concluded, "You need not worry about retirement. You'll be missionaries all your lives, and your supporting churches will continue to support you even in your retirement years."

Now, both points proved accurate enough for him. In his late fifties in 1984, he'd enjoyed a long effective missionary career. For his faithfulness, many churches rewarded him by continuing to support him when he reached retirement age.

122

And here's another thing. That missionary, now in his late 80s, is a millionaire. While giving us poor advice, he invested a good portion of his support in the stock market. Too bad he didn't share his stock market tips with us.

One of the most spiritual decisions you'll ever make as a missionary is to make adequate provisions for your retirement. And there are much better vehicles for retirement savings today.

You may think, "I will serve till I die."

My response is, "Are you sure you'll be able to do that? Be healthy enough to serve until you die?"

What if you suffer a stroke? Come down with cancer? What if fryou're seriously injured in a car accident? What if your spouse dies?

Then, there is the eventuality that even if you're doing God's work, the aging process reduces all of our abilities to function. It just may not be possible to serve as a missionary in your seventies.

I sit here today with a neurological problem that at age sixty-three has watched my right bicep waste away, robbing me of full function of my arm.

Are you sure you'll be able to do that?

Seven Components of Adequate Provision

There are **seven financial components** in successfully navigating the missionary life:

1. First, secure enough funds for your arrival and setup costs on the field.

2. Make sure you possess enough support to meet the needs of your spouse and children.

3. Stay out of debt! Don't throw away missions money on high interest credit cards.

4. Build an emergency fund for the unexpected. I encourage missionaries to keep six months support in reserve for unforeseen circumstances.

5. Put a little money aside each month into a travel fund for return trips back home. Churches fatigue at continual requests by their missionaries for money to purchase airline tickets.

6. Set aside a portion of your budget for ministry projects. Outside of special gifts for specific projects, stay within your budget. This keeps you from depriving yourself of adequate funds for living expenses.

7. Last, invest wisely to serve sufficiently into your advancing years of life. If you start in your 20s or 30s, a small monthly contribution towards retirement can reap enormous benefits.

 Sail On

What type of support do you currently possess to meet your needs? Are you under-supported? Adequately supported? Or fully-funded?

 True North

Take a lesson from the ants, you lazybones. Learn from their ways and become wise! Though they have no prince or governor or ruler to make them work, they labor hard all summer, gathering food for the winter.

Proverbs 6:6-8

Wealth from get-rich-quick schemes quickly disappears; wealth from hard work grows over time.

Proverbs 13:11

Good planning and hard work lead to prosperity, but hasty shortcuts lead to poverty.

Proverbs 21:5

The wise have wealth and luxury, but fools spend whatever they get.

Proverbs 21:20

 Light House

Raising your support and spending it is one of the most spiritual decisions you'll make. How you handle money reveals your attitude towards God and that which he entrusts to you; your family, ministry, health, and future.

Even when your frustrated, you can smile.

Survival Tip #10

Don't Let Your Calling Become a Culling

There is, one knows not what sweet mystery about the sea, whose gently awful stirrings seem to speak of some hidden soul beneath.

— Herman Melville
Moby Dick

David was now in great danger because all his men were very bitter about losing their sons and daughters, and they began to talk of stoning him.
But David found strength in the Lord his God.

I Samuel 30:6

126

JEFF, MY SOUTH AFRICAN FRIEND, loves to sail. In his catamaran, he's sailed up and down the coasts of Africa for decades. Once during our many conversations, I asked him why he enjoyed sailing so much. His answer sobered my estimation of not only sailing, but my walk with God too.

"It's in the ocean, I find my soul," he said.

Jeff tolerated little foolishness on the open waters by those accompanying him on his voyages. He pointed this out to me one day during coffee at Sonia's Café—can see it like it was yesterday—as he shared in his raspy-voiced words.

"Don, many people feel called to the ocean. They're intrigued by the water, the wave, and the wonder of it all. So they learn how to sail. They train, get certified, and embark on their sailing."

Then abruptly changing tone and posture, he continued, "But after a while, they lose the very thing they thought they loved. Some lose their lives too."

"It's like the culling of a herd of elephants I once saw as a young boy up in the Congo."

Jeff described a scene in the 1960s in Africa when he witnessed a culling of an elephant herd. He told of the awful necessity of reducing an elephant population, wreaking havoc upon farms and villages in the area where he lived as a boy.

"It was a horrible thing to witness," he concluded.

Then he went back to sailing.

"People forget to respect the sea," he said.

"They get careless. They know how to sail, but they forget what brought them to sailing. Their once seafaring love becomes just another thing to do rather than a passion; something to live for."

Sipping his coffee, he looked at me, erupting in self-discovery, "Doan! Many feel called to the ocean, but few let the ocean call to them. And, I suppose what happens to them is just like that elephant herd when the ocean removes them without mercy. They enter the waters with what they think they know about the ocean, only to drown in it."

Jeff proved a seaworthy sailor who literally sailed the seven seas of the world on his catamaran. Sailing was his calling, first love, and soulmate.

Then Jeff looked at me that day with a wrinkle of his nose and finished, "You've got to love the sea or leave the sea. There is no middle ground."

He chuckled, "Yah, middle ground, like there's any of that out there, anyway; you know ground."

That conversation made me think of the allure of missionary life that draws so many to cast off their ropes, hoist the anchor, and set sail for their mission fields. That unique unquantifiable calling of God.

The challenges,

Its dangers,

The rewards it offers,

The exhilarating lifestyle.

And the riptides of disappointment that wash so many out to sea, never to ride the waves of ministry again.

Called or Culled

Missionaries who thrive or languish in their missionary environments seem—at least to me—to fall into those two categories of people: Called or Culled.

Every missionary I've ever spoken with who thrives in their environment shares a touch from God. A unique calling. An unstoppable force that led them to forsake all for missionary work. Each calling is as unique as the missionaries themselves.

Called missionaries possess heart and stamina. They endeavor to understand the land, people, and culture God has called them to serve. Instead of working the people, moving them around like pieces on a ministry chessboard, they work with people.

Called missionaries learn what influences people in the culture they serve. What drives a culture, marking their unique identity as a people.

Above all else, called missionaries love Christ, endeavoring to touch souls with his love.

I don't say this is easy. Many times during my twenty-two years among the Zulu people in South Africa, those wonderful people saw too much of this missionary's desire to accomplish my God-stuff rather than experience Christ's love through me.

Yet, something happens out there in the depths of ministry, causing our callings to morph from determination to detriment. Missionaries too often lose their souls in the stormy waters of serving people. With honorable efforts, they get blown off course as the work culls back their soul.

Here are a few of the examples observed over the years that cull missionaries from their callings.

Ethnocentric Missionaries

Ethnocentricity is the inherent practice of viewing others solely through your own cultural background. Culled missionaries succumb to their ethnocentricities; the belief that their culture is superior. Lacking cultural relativism, [53] a cross-cultural worker can interpret people's attitudes and behaviors based on their own cultural personal perspective.

Colonialism marked an extreme form of this in Africa during the 18th and 19th century. Seven European countries in particular—Britain, France, Germany, Belgium, Spain, Portugal, and Italy—sought to control and subjugate hundreds of people groups around the world.

This followed by American "exceptionalism" stimulated more ethnocentrism among throngs of American missionaries that entered Africa. Much of the early missionary work conditioned Africans to approach Jesus from a Western perspective of worship.

Church buildings often looked European or American, as Africans dressed liked Western Christians. They sang English and German hymns translated into their languages rather than creating their own songs. And church structures became anything but African.

Let me give you a modest example of such a process.

The simple practice of using eating utensils—a knife, fork, and spoon—shows ethnocentricity in its most innocent form.

As an American, I learned to eat food using a fork with tines facing upwards. We used the knife mostly to cut. A spoon served more like a small shovel, scooping food to the mouth unless used to stir.

Silverware—as we called it in Minnesota—was a practical set of utensils used to accomplish a simple task, eating. When we moved to South Africa cutlery marked a different function.

Highly influenced by the British, cutlery upon a table was a more defined cultural expression by the white English-speaking population of South Africa.

Forks were set to the left of the plate. Usually, two knives sat to the right of the plate, and the soup spoon sat right of the knives. Knife blades faced inwards towards the plate.

Dessert forks and spoons laid above the plate with the fork prongs facing right and the spoon bowl facing left.[54] The side plate for bread and butter sat on the far left with the butter knife resting on top of the plate. Wine and water glasses sat on the top right above the knives and soup spoon.[55]

When eating, fork tines pointed downward rather than upward as in the United States. The knife was used to push food up onto the bottom of the fork which faced up. Food was brought to the mouth on an inverted fork.

I made bumbling ethnocentric errors the first few times eating with English South Africans by attempting to make comical remarks about their use of cutlery compared to my Minnesota upbringing.

A South African friend quickly set me in my place, calling it the proper—prăpăh—way to use a knife and fork. Today, as I use my knife and fork as learned in South Africa, friends occasionally make an ethnocentric remark like,

"Why don't you use your fork the right way?" Their jest makes me smile as their unintentional ethnocentrism blurts out.

Maybe the people of India have got it right. They don't use knives, spoons, or forks at all.

Anyway, all of this is mute since most culinary excursions in the United States end with the barbaric practice of using plasticware.

Once sitting in the Narita airport in Japan, an American woman scolded a Japanese server at a fast-food counter because they ran out of plastic forks and spoons.

The worker offered, "I'm sorry; we only have chopsticks left."

The traveler retorted, "What am I supposed to do with these?"

I mumbled under my breath, "Lady, you're in Japan; learn how to eat like 2 billion other people do in this world every day."

With that my wife, Kathy, whispered, "Sweetie, people can hear you."

Oops, did it again.

In its worst form, ethnocentricity is racist. That's how slavery developed; when a society deemed themselves better than another, subjugating others to serve their interests.

Christianity is exclusive, Jesus said, "No one can come to the Father except through me." John 14:6

That does not mean that a missionary's culture or way of worship is superior. Neither ought it imply that people are "saved, redeemed, born again, or Christianized" by doing church the way the missionary learned to do church.

Once, while working on my doctorate, an argument broke out between myself and my academic coach, who took issue with one of my writing projects.

I made the statement, "The American culture is not superior to any other culture." With that, he erupted with words on paper, rebuking me for my statement.

He talked about the Taliban, communism, socialism, cannibals in the jungles, Sasquatch, and Yeti legends. No joke, at one point, Bigfoot entered the conversation, too.

His coup de gras came in his last words, "Are you telling me our way of life is not superior to those people?"

I responded, "None of what you mention are actual cultures, but subcultures, economic systems, or legends. None of that makes a person less than another. The Gospel sees all people bound by sin and in need of a Savior, Jesus. With that, he approved my writing project.

Paul stated, "All have sinned and come short of the glory of God." Romans 3:10 KJV

All—everyone—finds an equal footing in God's view regarding missing the mark God set for us before sin entered this old world. All cultures fall short of God's intended purposes for them. No culture stands above another as superior.

Read the Minor Prophets. God judges all the nations. Matthew 25:31-46, Revelations 19:17-21

In missionary work, ethnocentric ministry is a belief and practice that— for example—Africa people must worship God in American style buildings, dressed in suits and ties for men, dresses for the women, and sing worship songs with little or no emotions.

Now you may think your American church members show emotions when singing during worship service, but you ain't been in a Zulu worship service!

As a Zulu man once said to me, "You Anglos can do music, but we Zulus are music."

Once during a worship service, Zulu believers danced and sang in worship. A visiting American came to me and said, "Make them stop that."

I replied, "If you nailed their feet to the concrete, they'd pull the slabs right out of the ground. Zulus dance. Zulus are dance. That's who they are."

Yet the African landscape is dotted with American and European church buildings filled with African believers who were taught the Nicaean Creed, Apostles Creed, Westminster Confession, or Articles of Faith held by Anglos. Taught everything except how to find Christ in their African mind and soul, and worship God in their own unique Africanism.

Missionary work often makes better adherents to the missionary's ways than followers of Jesus Christ. Pure missionary work is bringing people to Jesus and allowing God to—as my Zulu leaders used to say—grow them in the Way.

Culled

Culled missionaries drive sheep towards a way of doing Christianity rather than embracing the Way of Christianity. Rather than work with sheep, they work the sheep towards a desired ecclesiastical goal, a theological position, a system of worship, or an architectural structure.

Called

Called missionaries want to meet people where they're at. Accept them for who they are, and appreciate them whence they come, introducing them to the Great Shepherd.

For a called missionary, Jesus is everything.

"I give them eternal life, and they will never perish. No one can snatch them away from me..." Jesus—John 10:28

Marco Polo Missionaries

Marco Polo was a great explorer of the 13th century who explored Asia. The West knew little about China, Mongolia, and other nations of the East. Marco Polo's love of adventure, exploration and learning, helped introduced Asia to Western Europe.

Exploration is one of the many benefits of missionary life. For me, learning about the Zulus fascinated me. Studying the battlefields in Natal, South Africa, where with shields and spears, the Zulus charged British soldiers armed with Henry rifles and artillery guns captured my attention, helping me understand the Zulu people.

So too, exploring the Drakensberg Mountains in Natal, South Africa, standing above the clouds on the Amphitheater, next to—arguably—the highest waterfall in the world, was beyond my words to describe. The immense expanse and beauty; a canvas touched by God's paintbrush.

Or flying in a Piper Cub airplane over those same mountains to fish a friend's trout ponds for rainbow trout, and the next week stand with my family on the beaches of the Indian ocean marked a life I loved.

There's plenty of adventure in missionary life. Missionaries see the world and its people apart from the worn trails most tourists trod.

However, some missionaries talk mostly of their exploits. I've sat with missionaries for hours listening to them share their stories, hearing everything about anything except their ministries; the people they claim to love and serve.

Culled

Don't become just an explorer. Voyagers often consume themselves with finding the next new thing before enjoying that which they've already discovered.

Called

Called missionaries are adventurers, but they see their greatest venture in exploring the people they serve. They try to discover the beautiful uniqueness of their ethos and souls.

See the sites. Climb the mountains. Sail the seas. Enjoy the food and drinks. Oh, and don't forget about the sweets, chocolates, candies, and puddings too! The more a missionary enjoys the country they live in, the more likely ministry will become meaningful and fulfilling.

Most of all, relish the people. Living to help people find Jesus—a Lighthouse in a sea of human suffering—is the greatest adventure of all.

Wanderlust Missionaries

If you want to travel, missionary life is the ticket. Over my missionary career, I've visited twenty-five countries. From Machu Picchu in Peru, a Buddhist temple in Thailand, to the Roman Colosseum in Italy, and the list goes on. There's plenty of travel in the missionary life.

Chris Lautsbaugh—Missionary teacher and author with Youth With A Mission—notes, "Being a missionary carries a great cost, *but does have some benefits*. It is not all doom and gloom, complete with vows of poverty and poor fashion choices for clothing." [56]

Concerning travel, he blogs, "In today's day and age it is easy to benefit from one aspect of the missionary life—frequent travel. The nature of missions involves being traveling missionaries. We have left home to go somewhere." [57]

Yet, a word of caution here. The modern era of enjoying coffee in South Africa on Tuesday, and eating at your favorite restaurant in New Zealand on Friday, can—and often does—play havoc with the cross-cultural worker's mind and soul.

In the old days, missionaries packed their few belongings, boarded a ship, and set sail to a new home. They rarely, if ever, returned to the country of their births. Their arrivals to the field marked a burning of bridges to return to their home countries. In this, they settled quickly.

I met the grandsons of such missionaries, third-generation South Africans, during my many years in South Africa. When their grandparents arrived, South Africa became home. There was never any intention of returning to the country of their birth. They raised their children and their children's children in the land.

Settled, and in one place, they became South Africans.

I've found the constant departing and arriving from one country to the next both enjoyable and baneful in my missionary career. Constantly tearing myself between two countries, my family in Minnesota and my friends in South Africa, generated extreme mixtures of emotions.

Travel is the difficulty—almost impossibility—of settling one's mind, person, and family in any one place for the modern-day cross-cultural worker.

Understanding this challenge upfront helps to prepare you for missionary service.

Added to this are the challenges of travel in a COVID-19 world. The Coronavirus has changed the way will we do missions for years to come.

Culled

While traveling offers many benefits, it can take a huge toll too. Entry, return, and continual reentry back and forth between the country of ministry and the country of birth can prove disorienting. Many missionaries share this with me.

Adjustment disorders plague many missionaries as they move from one compartmentalized life to another, repeatedly interchanging their lifestyles.

One missionary shared, "It's like living in a chapter of a book. Reaching the end of one chapter, only to find your opening the next chapter in a whole new book unrelated to the last chapter in the previous book."

In this, many missionaries give up, longing for the way it was back home.

Called

A missionary once shared, "All my friends and family put together haven't seen as much of the world as me. I love that part of missionary life, but I never get my eyes off the real reason I travel so much."

Florence Nightingale Missionaries

Florence Nightingale was an English social reformer, statistician, and the founder of modern nursing. Nightingale came to prominence while serving as a manager and trainer of nurses during the Crimean War in which she organized care for wounded soldiers. [58]

Current-day missionaries around the world assist the sick and dying, making Herculean efforts to help them. Their sacrifices and acts of heroism rarely emerge in self-absorbed conflict-centered social media. Yet, did you know that a cure for HIV-AIDS may come through the work of missionaries?

Christianity Today notes some amazing things happening out in the world of medical missions. Missionaries are changing medicine across the world.

Take, for example, Mississippi pediatrician Hannah Gay. She has done something never accomplished before: She cured a baby born with the AIDS virus. Gay is not just a pediatrician but also a former Southern Baptist missionary to Ethiopia. She has made just one of many significant discoveries by current and former medical missionaries worldwide. [59]

Ever hear of Dennis Burkitt? As a medical missionary in the 1950s and 60s, he discovered a cancer while investigating jaw tumors in Ugandan children. The cancer is named after him; "Burkitt's lymphoma." [60]

"Christian-inspired missionaries and nationals [have] made huge contributions to global health," said Ray Martin, director of Christian Connection for International Health.[61]

A cure for cancer might come from a missionary in a 3rd world country rather than a clinical laboratory in the West.

Christianity Today again notes in their January 10, 2017 edition the contributions of three missionary doctors in consideration of the $500,000 Gerson L'Chaim prize for outstanding Christian medical service:

Dr. Stephen Foster, in Angola for 38 years, headed a growing medical center. In a country of 12 million and almost no modern healthcare, internships help upgrade new Angolan physicians—training 24 M.D's, each one to see 4,000 patients a year.

Dr. William Rhodes, in Kenya, a reconstructive surgeon, has performed 15,000 surgeries. He sought the prize to help him mentor two young Kenyan surgeons and thus double the hospital's operations. The money also would expand services outside his region and buy much-needed basic surgical equipment.

Dr. John Spurrier, in rural Zambia, where the money could improve HIV care for 4,000 patients in rural areas, add electricity and water for his mission hospital, and provide suitable housing for staff.[62]

Helping the sick in South Africa brought great fulfillment for me, but years of watching people—particularly children—die of AIDS in South Africa wreaked havoc upon my mind and soul. Serving the suffering ground me down to disfunction, leading to my PTSD.

Culled

Some say I am weak, unspiritual, or too wrapped up in myself. Perhaps this is so. But here I am, still seeing the eyes of dozens of little children taking their last breath, dying from AIDS. Images I can't shake regardless of the amount of prayer or distraction I direct towards them.

> Serving the sick can exact a high price on missionaries.

Missionary, you must beware of the high cost of serving the sick. It's the noblest of missionary services, but it also exacts a high price on its workers. Serving those in acute distress often leads to a very troubled you. Trouble that can penetrate your soul, rendering you to a feelingless numbing existence.

Called

Helping preserve a life that otherwise might perish is one of the greatest vocations of a missionary. To know that, "Unless I'd been there, this child, person, or community might have perished," brings ultimate fulfillment.

Such a sense of accomplishment can help a missionary keep going in the most difficult of days.

But regular detachment and R & R are necessary to survive in conditions where human suffering is high.

Self-care and soul-care are top priorities in avoiding becoming the next culled missionary. It's an absolute must in preventing burnout and other debilitating illnesses.

Finding a spiritual guide, mental health worker, or friend is a must. Group sessions with other missionaries struggling with the same issues can build resistance to mental illnesses.

Here's the thing. *Souls helping other suffering souls often experience vicarious trauma; mental suffering of those you're helping.*

Expect it. Prepare for it. Learn to deal with it. But please don't ignore it.

Called or Culled Missionary

Perhaps one sizable difference between becoming another missionary casualty lies in that which motivated you to missionary service.

Obeying the command is essential. Jesus commanded, "Therefore, go and make disciples of all the nations, baptizing them in the name of the Father and the Son and the Holy Spirit. Teach these new disciples to obey all the commands I have given you." Matthew 28:19-20a

As followers of Christ, we bear Christ's command to produce disciples. This work should take place everywhere, and in everything we do.

Following a desire to help people is good too. "Take delight in the Lord, and he will give you your heart's desires." Psalm 37:4

This Scripture is sometimes quoted by people considering missionary service. I want to help people, and God has enable me to do so.

A special touch by God is perfect. The missionary calling is as diverse as missionaries themselves. Every experience is unique. Each shares a unique touch of God to enter missionary service. Yet each bears a similarity of answering a call.

As Isaiah responded to the Lord's words, "Whom shall I send, and who will go for us? Then said I, Here am I; send me." Isaiah 6:8 KJV

What moves you? In your missionary calling, God will move in unique and diverse ways to launch you into the depths of missionary service.[63]

Returning to what motivated you into missionary service in the first place may help you remain in missionary service when it gets difficult. To wait until God moves you towards a new assignment or stay in your current location.

 Sail On

How are you caring for yourself, your family, and other members of your team? Long-term ministry depends upon your viability as a person physically, mentally, and spiritually.

Not the self-care so prevalent in this age of "taking care of number one." That kind of self-care puts you at the center of your self-sufficiency. The self-care needed for longevity marks itself by continual dependence upon God's presence.

True North

For we are not fighting against flesh-and-blood enemies, but against evil rulers and authorities of the unseen world, against mighty powers in this dark world, and against evil spirits in the heavenly places.

Ephesians 6:12

Guard your heart above all else, for it determines the course of your life.

Proverbs 4:23

Search me, O God, and know my heart; test me and know my anxious thoughts. Point out anything in me that offends you, and lead me along the path of everlasting life.

Psalm 139:23-24

 Light House

Make sure you're able to finish your journey. Learn to care for yourself. Don't allow your sails to fill beyond their capacity to endure the trip.

Remember, *what does your calling matter if you allow yourself to be dashed upon the rocks of missionary service?*

Always point your soul towards God. And, in your darkest hours, remember,

"The Lord is your fortress; your God is the mighty rock where you hide."

Psalm 94:22

"A smile can brighten a dreary day."

A Poem by Kurt Hearth

Survival Tip #11

Take a Sabbath Before the Sabbath Takes You.

If you don't take the sabbath, the sabbath will take you.

Carey Nieuwhof

If you don't make time for your wellness, you will be forced to make time for your illness.

Pinterest – Unknown

On the seventh day God had finished his work of creation, so he rested from all his work.

Genesis 2:2

After sending them home, he went up into the hills by himself to pray. Night fell while he was there alone.

Jesus – Matthew 14:23

RECENTLY, I POSED A QUESTION to the Global Member Care Network—GMCN—of which I am a member. There are over four thousand members in this group on Facebook alone. The participants represented thousands of care providers from dozens of nationalities and countries, providing care for cross-cultural workers all over the world. The question was,

"What is the biggest spiritual deficit in the lives of missionaries you encounter?"

The most repeated answer surprised me. Care providers asserted that the largest spiritual deficit of missionaries *was their failure to take adequate sabbaths*; periods of respite, timeouts, and seasons of redirection away from missionary duties and work. Several caregivers used the term **Sabbath's Rest**.

Hosts of missionary caregivers noted that many cross-cultural workers who reach out to them did so in *fragile, depleted states*. Workers regularly came to them emotionally limp, physically diminished, and spiritually tepid.

When I look back at my own missionary life, probably the most grievous of my personal neglects was failing to plan for regular sabbaths – short times of rest – and the occasional Sabbatical for much longer periods of rest and reflection.

Rest—outside of sleep—rarely surfaced in my schedules. While on the field, there were lessons to teach, buildings to construct, languages to learn, leaders to train, and a longer list of sub-points to follow each focal point.

When on home assignment back in the States – a supposed period of R & R—once the plane hit the tarmac, I was off to perform my duties. There were studies to attend to, academic degrees to earn, supporters needing a personal report, family members to see, medical needs to attend to, temporary housing to secure, national meetings to go to, and 10s of thousands of miles to drive in a short time.

Within ten years of my approval as a missionary, I was physically exhausted and mentally fatigued. Both a Sabbatical—leave from my duties—and sabbath's rests—days off—screamed for attention.

Sabbath's Rest

There is a principle marked out in Scriptures that commands systematic, regular withdrawal from activities to focus upon rest. It is a largely ignored principle by missionaries who mark their lifestyles by continual travel, fundraising, and work.

When overlooked, the continual push to do results in personal wreckage scattered along the shorelines of ministry. No ship stays at sea continuously without dry-docking occasionally for inspection, cleaning, and repair of the hull.[64] And,

God Was Pretty Clear About the Sabbath:

Remember to observe the Sabbath day by keeping it holy.

You have six days each week for your ordinary work, but the seventh day is a Sabbath day of **rest** dedicated to the Lord your God. On that day, no one in your household may do any work. This includes you, your sons and daughters, your male and female servants, your livestock, and any foreigners living among you.

For in six days the Lord made the heavens, the earth, the sea, and everything in them; but on the seventh day he **rested**.

That is why the Lord blessed the Sabbath day and set it apart as holy.

Exodus 20:8-11

The word 'rested' in Genesis 2:2 comes from the Hebrew word 'שָׁבַת shabath' and is in the Qal stem. It means to cease from labor and rest. Cease from labor and rest; what does that mean for us on Sunday?

During my years in South Africa, I'd slip up to Israel unaccompanied by throngs of other sightseers. It always intrigued me to watch an entire nation shut down from nightfall on Friday until nightfall on Saturday.

The Sabbath applied to more than only people too:

While Moses was on Mount Sinai, the Lord said to him,

'Give the following instructions to the people of Israel. When you have entered the land I am giving you, the land itself must observe a Sabbath rest before the Lord every seventh year.

For six years you may plant your fields and prune your vineyards and harvest your crops,

but during the seventh year the land must have a Sabbath year of complete rest. It is the Lord's Sabbath. Do not plant your fields or prune your vineyards during that year.

And don't store away the crops that grow on their own or gather the grapes from your unpruned vines. The land must have a year of complete rest.

But you may eat whatever the land produces on its own during its Sabbath. This applies to you, your male and female servants, your hired workers, and the temporary residents who live with you.

Your livestock and the wild animals in your land will also be allowed to eat what the land produces.

Leviticus 25:1-7

146

The Sabbath is referred to often in agricultural terms throughout the Old Testament. It's the concept of *resting the fields*. Allowing adequate rest so the nutrients and goodness can return to the soil.

Any crop farmer will explain that you can't plant the same crop on the same field year after year. Crops need rotation, planting different crops on a field from one year to the next. This ensures the soil maintains its goodness to produce a healthy crop the next year.

So too, people need Sabbatical Rests to ensure body, soul, and spirit nutrients keep us healthy and productive.

And let us remember the ultimate purpose of the Old Testament Sabbath.

"Tell the people of Israel: 'Be careful to keep my Sabbath day, for the Sabbath is a sign of the covenant between me and you from generation to generation. *It is given so you may know that I am the Lord, who makes you holy.*"

Exodus 31:13 Emphasis Mine

Whoa! Wait a minute!

That's in the Old Testament. We don't do that today. Anyways, Jesus is Lord of the Sabbath, so that means it doesn't apply to us today. Right?

Yes, the Sabbath is an Old Testament principle. It's also emphasized in the New Testament. The Christian Church marked the first day of the week—Sunday—as its day of worship, and I doubt that involved all the activities we surround ourselves with today outside our two hours of worship on Sunday.

Jesus is Lord of the Sabbath. As Lord of the Sabbath—Matthew 12:8—he had the right to overrule the Pharisee's traditions and regulations concerning it. Jesus owned the Sabbath. The Sabbath did not own him.

Ever ask yourself what the Pharisees were doing hiking about on the Sabbath when they accused Jesus of breaking it? Makes me chuckle.

147

Yet, the Gospel records Jesus often escaping the demanding needs of people to get alone with God. To meditate, to pray, to take a deep spiritual breath, and to rest.

Our Savior needed regular intervals of rest. What does that say about us today who run back and forth in our busy activities?

Others hold that Jesus is the fulfillment of our Sabbath's Rest. Our relationship in Christ makes the old law of the Sabbath no longer binding today.[65]

Ok, but none of that removes the principle nor the necessity of rest. Rest over the constant activity of moving, traveling, raising support, raising special money for projects and buildings, feeding the hungry, caring for the poor, flying back and forth to our home countries just to repeat and do it all over again. Jetlag alone cries for a Sabbath.

Missionary, when do you ever rest? EVER?

I doubt furlough and home assignments provide much of a Sabbath's Rest.

So, when do you actually take time to rest?

To give your soul time to breathe.

To reflect upon the God's workings in your life?

When?

Missionary Sundays

My Sundays in South Africa began early in the mornings. We traveled out to several churches in different locations in a vehicle without air-conditioning.

Upon arriving home late in the afternoon, we'd enjoy a meal as a family, then followed by a nap for me. In the evening, we took our young sons for a walk. Most missionary Sundays marked a day of exhaustion, not a day of rest.

Missionary Mondays

Mondays were hardly a day off or time for rest either. There were people to see, places to go, and living in Africa—always—lines to stand in waiting for goods and services.

Once, while living in South Africa, my friend Keith brought this to my attention. He asked, "Don, when was the last time you took a holiday? I mean, you take no time off for Kathy, the boys, and yourself. Do you?"

Earlier we'd entered South Africa. Africa was still new to me. The Zulu language still fascinated me. The Drakensberg mountains presented continual breathtaking views. Every day felt like a vacation in those early days.

But my sons battled every day in school, adapting to a South African style of education and making friends in a new culture. Kathy struggled to navigate a whole new lifestyle and keep up with my pace.

In all my excited busyness to learn a language, explore a new location, develop relationships with African people, live in an unfamiliar country, and share the Good News of Jesus Christ, there was rarely any downtime time, much less time to spend relaxing my mind and developing my relationships.

MKs See It

It's a common complaint heard many times over forty years of missionary life and pastoral work.

I wish dad and mom would have spent more time with us than at the church, clinic, or school.

Same from missionary wives, too.

I wish he'd spend more time with me than them.

While in Bible college years ago, meals in the cafeteria spent in the company of MK's revealed a familiar theme. Whenever a complaint arose, it often circled around the prevailing thought that missionary work came before missionary kids.

149

It's my observation that in this area—with MKs—younger missionary parents today do much better than their predecessors in recognizing the needs of their MKs, spending more time and effort to help them adjust to the challenges of growing up in a missionary environment.

Attitudes Affirm It

Years ago, there was a popular saying spoken by many who busied themselves doing "God's work." In a braggadocios tone, they claimed, "I'd rather burn out for God than rust out."

My thought was, "What's the difference? Either way, you're out."

We credit the saying to Amy Carmichael, the great Protestant Christian missionary to India. But her 55 years of service and the many books she wrote points more towards a woman who took considerable Sabbath Rests amid her demanding missionary endeavors. Her continual battle from childhood neuralgia often confined her to bed for weeks at a time.

A busy missionary put it like this, "I'd rather go down swinging than just sitting on the porch."

I asked him, "Of the two options—going down swinging or just sitting—which reflects your greatest struggle?"

"What do you mean," he said.

For the next hour we discussed that God's call in a missionary's life was far beyond mere activity. That conversation discovered a lack of attendance to spiritual disciplines, family time, and personal care in his life.

Missionary Burnout

The World Health Organization defines burnout as,

A syndrome conceptualized as resulting from chronic workplace stress that has not been successfully managed.

They characterize it by three dimensions:

- Feelings of energy depletion or exhaustion;
- Increased mental distance from one's job, or feelings of negativism or cynicism related to one's job; and
- Reduced professional efficacy.[66]

> Missionary burnout is more of a drain out.

I think missionary burnout is more of a drain out than burnout. When missionaries deplete themselves. They run out of mind, soul, and body to spend needed energies in their relationships, marriage, family, and ministry. Avoiding missionary drain out requires discipline and planning. But for many, it's just drip, drip, drip…

Missionary Stress

A few years ago, while living in South Africa, I took the Holmes-Rahe Stress Scale. This test was developed in 1967 after examining the records of 5,000 medical patients to determine whether stressful events caused their illnesses. Patients were asked to tally a list of 43 life events based on a relative score.[67]

Each life event was given a numerical score. Here are a few examples:

- Death of a spouse 100
- Death of a family member 63
- Personal injury or illness 53
- Business readjustment 39
- Change in responsibilities at work 29
- Change in residence 20
- Change in school 20
- Change in church activities 19
- Change in social activities 19

151

The American Institute of Stress explains the results:

- **150 points or less** | a relatively low amount of life change and a low susceptibility to stress-induced health breakdown.
- **150 to 300 points** | 50% chance of health breakdown in the next 2 years.
- **300 points or more** | 80% chance of health breakdown in the next 2 years, according to the Holmes-Rahe statistical prediction model.[68]

When I took my test, I scored over 700. That didn't include:

- The little Zulu girl who died in my arms from AIDS that week.
- A friend who was gunned down in a robbery that month.
- My Neurologist in Pietermaritzburg who was poisoned to death over a lover's quarrel.
- Having our pickup truck stolen the month before.

The test solidified for me the reason we—mostly me—struggled so much the last five years of our ministry in South Africa. The same is true for many missionaries.

Most missionaries land high of the Holmes Rahe Stress Test; around 600. And first-term missionaries can average as high as 900! [69] Is it any wonder that so many of us are sick and struggling?

A Missionary Friend

Just this past week, I listened to a missionary share his story with a Sunday morning congregation. He began with, "I've never shared this before in a church."

The man and his wife worked in an all Muslim country. After a furlough, he suffered a nervous breakdown just before returning to the field. While laying in an ER waiting room for doctors to commit him to a mental health unit, a pastor friend encouraged him to take, as he described it, "A year with no work, just spending time with Jesus." A true Sabbatical. That, he did.

For a year he prayed, read the Scriptures, poured over the pages of Sarah Young's *Jesus Calling*, and dozens of other spiritual journals. The result? Ten years later, he and his wife still serve the Muslim people in that country.

Examples from the Scriptures

Many people in the Bible suffered from high levels of stress, too. Their examples can help us cope with our stresses today. Some thrived despite their pressures, while others succumbed to it. The examples are there, and they are worth studying.

Paul—first missionary to the Gentiles—listed some of his stressful situations in 2 Corinthians 11:23-28:

- Worked hard, struggled, and toiled
- Imprisoned repeatedly
- Beaten, whipped, and stoned
- Constantly on the move
- Shipwrecked
- In danger from his own people; countrymen
- Both the city and country covered with danger
- Risk from 'false brothers'
- Sleep deprivation
- Hungry and thirsty
- Cold and lacked clothing
- Pressure for his concern of the churches [70]

Reading the book of Acts, you also find that early Christians faced a variety of stressors:

- Physical disabilities and sickness
- False accusations
- Opposition by religious leaders
- Lies and criticisms from other believers towards them
- Weather delays halting travel
- Headwinds slowing travel
- Theological differences within the church
- Sharp personal disagreements
- Riots
- Limited financial resources
- Evacuations
- Snakebites and sicknesses
- Legal action against them [71]

King Saul yielded to his stresses while King David lived above them, ah, well, most of the time. There's the whole Bathsheba thing, and the numbering of the people.

Most of the Disciples dealt well with the extreme pressures dropped upon them for believing in Christ. We tend to focus on the most positive aspects of their sufferings for encouragement.

I think many teachers in Christian circles over-spiritualize the plight of people in the Bible without considering the human consequences they produced.

Yes, Joseph's ending in Genesis is a great story of God's faithfulness and purpose in our struggles. It's a testimony of prevailing faith even in the most difficult of trials. But, I doubt... he was happy and energetic just after his brothers threw him in the pit, stole his clothes, and sold him into slavery. Joseph learned to trust God and adjusted, but... he suffered immensely. Let's not forget that.

The stress of King Solomon's rule led him into poor choices maritally and spiritually that damaged the kingdom for future generations.

It took Moses 40 years in the wilderness—sabbatical—to recover from the murder he committed in Egypt and reach a level of spiritual maturity and mental competence that allowed him to lead a nation.

Jeremiah—the Weeping Prophet—likely never overcame the pressures produced when conveying God's words to a doomed, unbelieving nation.

A passage of the Targum to Isaiah quoted by Jolowicz states that when Isaiah fled from his pursuers and took refuge in a tree, the tree was sawn in half, and the prophet's blood spurted forth. [72]

Myriads of examples occur in the Bible of God's people buckling under stress. It helps remind us that life is a struggle, and the need for respite it real.

COVID-19

When COVID-19 broke unto the world scene, missionaries either returned to their sending countries or hunkered down amidst the limited mobility that Stay-At-Home orders demanded. Some missionaries we Zoomed with during this time lived holed up in apartments in megacities.

Others in third-world countries faced harsh restrictions for leaving their residencies. In many places, aggressive police and military tactics enforced government mandates.

Newly arrived missionaries got hit the hardest. Arriving to their fields only six months before the Covid pandemic broke out, they found themselves locked down in their new countries

I've communicated with several new missionaries who were well past 100 days in lockdown as I wrote these words. Except for one trip a week to purchase food by only one family member, everyone else was confined to their homes. Imagine living in a small apartment with three children and not being permitted to leave.

A COVID's Rest

After speaking with many missionaries, a common theme emerged. Missionary after missionary felt that the Coronavirus provided them with forced rest and reflection. The consensus was that the pause in activity and cessation from the urge for continuous motion was a good thing in the middle of a dreadful event.

Even for myself—when faced with restricted movement—initial reactions did not focus upon God. Too much TV and social media turned into a disciplined approach towards spiritual disciplines and prayer.

How Do I Take a Sabbatical?

Again, a Sabbatical is a pulling away from the work for an extended season of refocus, redirection, and refreshing. Alternatively, sabbaths are regular repeated intervals–preferably weekly–of rest and relaxations. I like to call this The Five Rs: rest, relaxation, refocus, redirection, and refreshing. They are all necessary for longevity in cross-cultural service.

> The Five R's: rest, relaxation, refocus, redirection, and refreshing.

Objections to taking sabbaths and sabbaticals often revolves around the "how's" and "what ifs."

How will I find the time?
How will we pay for it?
What if my supporters think I'm lazy?
What if my agency doesn't agree?
What if the work suffers while I'm gone?
What will I do during that time?
How do I begin even contemplating taking a sabbath?

There're plenty of reasons to find for not taking these intervals of rest. One far overshadowing reason for practicing sabbaths and sabbaticals is to ensure perseverance. To finish well in the pursuit of your calling. *What does your calling matter if you don't finish what God set out before you?*

Taking a sabbath requires planning and forethought. Here's some principles laid out by Safe Place Ministries:[73]

Identify When a Sabbatical is Needed. It's far better to plan proactively rather than reactively. Preparing for a sabbatical is necessary for longevity. When someone serves extensively, a sabbath is probably in order.

There's something about the 7s in the Bible. The seventh day of rest and resting the fields in the seventh year are just two examples. Ideally, a cross-cultural worker should take a full one-year sabbatical—home assignment and fund raising doesn't count—after every seven years of service.

Also, if you experience severe trauma or difficulties, look at taking a sabbatical. Severe incidents have a way of grinding us down. A season of unrelated activity often helps us to live and serve another day.

Define your time. How will this period differ from a time of care, or leave of absence? A leave of absence, LOA, is a reactive approach to a condition that is acute. A few examples are depression, moral problems, or health issues.

A sabbatical is a planned season of REST; reviving, relaxing, and restoration. An LOA is a reaction of removing an unhealthy person from duties.

Prepare and implement your sabbath. Begin organizing the tangibles for your sabbath at least 3 months out. Consider,

Where will you stay during your sabbatical?

What will you engage in that will focus you upon rest?

Take up a hobby, learn to play an instrument, enroll in a class, write, walk, explore, or perhaps take in the amazing beauties of the mountains or oceans.

Will you travel, and if so, where to? I recommend leisure travel only, not furlough-fundraising, reporting travel. Don't run from here to there spending most of your time traveling. *Beware that you don't spend your sabbatical in intensity. Seek calmness.* Here are some operative words:

Rest.
Care.
Reflect.
Pause.
Listen.
Play.
Learn.

Allow spiritual nutrients to seep back into your soul. Wait for a vibrancy to return to your demeanor. Tarry until a sense of purpose reignites your spirit.

And attend to your health too. See a doctor. Get a physical. Just get better. Improve your lifestyle during this time.

Focus on your relationships. Take those long walks together. Play with your children or grandkids. Enjoy your pets. Hug your aging parents. Enrich yourself by experiencing those around you.

And most of all, take a big breath. Exhale your doubts, discouragements, and despairs pouring over the Scriptures expecting God's spirit to revive you.

God's Rest, Our Sabbath

Scripture tells us that "God blessed the seventh day and declared it holy, *because it was the day when he rested from all his work of creation.*" Genesis 2:2-3

I doubt God got tired. So why did God need rest? Perhaps it was an example of how much we—his creation—need to rest and refocus.

What I am saying is, "If God rested after working for six days, then maybe we should too?"

A Sabbath's Rest refocuses us upon God's creation. Relaxing ourselves to contemplate the cosmos can help take our minds off ourselves, placing them solely upon the immensity of God. The sun, moon, the spectacular beauty of the planets of this solar system, the billions of stars in the Milky Way, and the trillions of stars in the universe cause awe.

Wow, God, you do magnificent work.

The smallest of organisms in our oceans needed to sustain life generates wonderment when seeing God's attention to every detail.

Sitting on the porch in front of the lake, appreciating the surroundings, creates an attitude of gratitude.

Sabbath Rests help us contemplate God's outstanding work in our lives. Paul told the young Timothy,

> And I am certain that God who began the good work within you, will continue his work until it is finally finished on the day when Christ Jesus returns.

> Philippians 1:6

What is it that God is working in you? Ever think about that much? God, what are you doing in my life right now?

I know that when I'm discouraged or lonely, that kind of contemplation takes me away from centering upon myself, refocusing me to center upon God.

A sabbath's rest helps us accomplish more—not less. Matthew J. Edmund M.D., in his article *The Power of Rest* in Psychology Today, notes that geniuses like Einstein and G. H. Hardy 'worked' only four hours a day. They recognized what science now shows—that the body as an information system always rebuilds and renews.[74]

Edmund argued that human creative activity, whether related to 'brain' or 'brawn,' is restricted by fatigue that is biologically limited. Both mind and body need systematic downtime to operate efficiently when in mind or motion.[75]

Missionary, could it be—just maybe—the reason you're unable to accomplish or perform at the levels you desire is because you don't allow sufficient rest periods in your life?

Respite away from the drive to go all the time?

Quiet times to relax and refresh the mind?

159

Spiritual moments with God to rejuvenate your soul?

A single missionary woman shared, "Sometimes I'm so busy serving the Lord that I spend little time with God."

Note Jesus' words to the ever-busy Martha:

> But Martha was distracted by the big dinner she was preparing. She came to Jesus and said, 'Lord, doesn't it seem unfair to you that my sister just sits here while I do all the work? Tell her to come and help me.'

> But the Lord said to her, 'My dear Martha, you are worried and upset over all these details! There is only one thing worth being concerned about. Mary has discovered it, and it will not be taken away from her.'

> Luke 10:40-42

Martha worried while Mary worshipped. Martha fretted as Mary soaked in the company of Jesus. We know the story, don't we? Martha never applies to us because we all believe we're Mary.

Ah, isn't that a punch in the gut busy missionary? That some quiet do-nothing time with God may accomplish more than your mightiest efforts for him?

Finding time to rest and worship proves difficult. However, it is essential to keeping our minds, souls, and bodies in peak condition to meet the demanding challenges of missionary life and work.

Sail On

Write down the last five Sabbath's Rests you took. You know, a short period of downtime to relax, uncoil your brain and exhale from the busyness of it all. Your last five times. Come on now:

1. _____

2. _____

3. _____

4. _____

5. _____

Can't do it, can you?

Ok, let's try it again. Give this some thought. If there were no limits to your schedule, hindrances, or finances, what one step might you take forward towards a genuine personal sabbath plan? One first step? What is it?

_____

_____

_____

_____

_____

_____

Now, contemplate a sabbatical you need to take. A long period of detachment from regular duties for refocusing, reviving, rejuvenating, relaxing, renewing, and then to re-enter your ministry.

Dream a bit here. What might your sabbatical look like?

 True North

Then Jesus said, "Let's go off by ourselves to a quiet place and rest awhile." He said this because there were so many people coming and going that Jesus and his apostles didn't even have time to eat.

Mark 6:31

So there is a special rest still waiting for the people of God. For all who have entered into God's rest have rested from their labors, just as God did after creating the world.

Hebrews 4:9-10

 Light House

Take a Sabbath before it takes you. If you wait too long, when a forced Sabbath comes upon you, it will break your bones. Far better to keep your vessel fit and in good repair than in the dry docks of ruin. Your choice.

And please remember to smile. Will yah? Huh?

Survival Tip #12

Rethink Your View of Suffering

The Call to Missionary Service is a Call to Suffering.

TAKE A MOMENT TO THINK about your calling to missions. The event, process, or connection that led—or currently leads—you to contemplate entering missionary life. How might you describe it?

My calling to cross-cultural service is a call to _____. I've heard many descriptors of this calling and used many of them myself. But did you ever hear anyone describe the missionary calling as a call to suffering?

The Apostle Paul described it this way, "And everyone who wants to live a godly life in Christ Jesus *will suffer persecution.*" 2 Timothy 3:12

Does missionary life demand us to live a godly life in Christ Jesus? It absolutely does, doesn't it? *Therefore, the missionary life is among many other things, a call to suffering.*

A call to suffering. Hum… You hear little about that in sterilized classrooms of training centers. Few online missiology and cross-cultural training courses challenge us to suffer while sitting in familiar settings staring into a computer screen. Yet every missionary I know, endures persecution and suffering.

Thayer's Greek Lexicon describes the word 'persecution'—diōkō—as meaning anything to make one run or flee, put to flight, harass, trouble, or molest. Paul uses this word literally and figuratively in his writings.[76]

Let's rephrase the question. What harassing trouble or molestation do you foresee coming during your missionary service?

See where I'm going here?

Sometimes suffering is just life. We live in a fallen world that's in continual decay. When awful things happen to others, "Well, that's just life." But when those same events pour out upon my life, the tendency is to respond, "But God, why me?"

Harassments, suffering, and persecution can come in anxieties, OCD tendencies, mental health issues, and physical afflictions. Car accidents, food poisoning, malaria, dengue fever, and other afflictions cause a missionary to suffer.

As I write this very sentence, a missionary woman whom we served with in South Africa for twenty years battles for her life afflicted with COVID-19.

Having recently returned home from Africa to see her grandchildren and family, she now lays unconscious on a ventilator.

Hostile people who reject the message and Person we try to proclaim often forces suffering upon us.

Some missionaries sacrifice their very lives for the Gospel. I've known a few of these heroes of the faith.

And let's not forget about the spiritual suffering. Our battle is mostly against the powers of this dark world. Ephesians 6:12 While sharing Jesus, teaching the Scriptures, helping those little orphans, caring for the sick, and trying to uplift the downcast, the enemy will strike. Count on it.

Missionary, please understand this. While the missionary calling leads to many wonderful fulfilling rich experiences and rewards, it is primarily a call to suffer.

The Safest Place is in God's Will, Really?

I remember—as a young missionary—listening to a missions conference speaker. Don't know what exactly qualified that individual to wear the label 'Mission's Conference Speaker.' Perhaps, his yearly trips to Mazatlán gave him his immense experience to address the seasoned group of missionaries sitting before him that evening.

He stated, "Missionaries, the safest place to be is in God's will."

A quick perusal of the Bible showed that statement false. Read the end of the eleventh chapter of Hebrews. See what happened to all those folk mentioned there who arguably died in the center of God's will.

Take a look at Christ's disciples. Didn't end so well for them; if safe is the measurement of being in the center of God's will. Hear little of that kind of cross-bearing cost-counting preparation these days. Do we?

My 40 years of missionary and pastoral service testifies that often the most dangerous place to be is in the center of God's will. Especially for missionaries.

I think about a dedicated missionary couple out in Somewhere, Africa—actual events—when during one dark, horrible evening, men entered their home, bound the missionary husband and gang raped the missionary wife.

Try preaching the power of positive thinking, sow a seed of faith, believe it and claim it flim-flam drivel to her.

Or another missionary couple in their first year of service in Somewhere, South America. While shopping in the local market she experienced the same horrible personal violating theft when 5 men took from her that which can never return.

Or, when two men in a pickup truck brandishing automatic weapons in Somewhere, Central America forced a van load of Missionary Kids and their counselors off the road. After murdering the adult missionary driver, they robbed the group leaving them stranded.

In our missions agency's headquarters, hang the pictures of career missionaries who died in missionary service. Among the many portraits hangs three in particular.

On May 4, 1985, Thomas Brown was shot and killed by gunmen at his home in Puente Piedra, Peru. The murder occurred in front of his dear wife Fran. As young missionaries, Kathy and I listened to Fran share her story at a missionary retreat in the mountains of Colorado.

Several years later Fran died of cancer. Both their pictures hang on our missionary wall of fame; the cost of their missionary service immense.

Another picture is of a gracious 82-year-old elderly missionary, living in a remote part of Brazil. The remarkable earthly life of Marjorie Browning ended abruptly on November 12, 2014. According to his published confession, a 16-year-old man—boy really—struck and killed Marjorie during a burglary.[77]

Recently, sitting with a missionary couple entering their 20th year of service in Eastern Europe, the missionary wife revealed her disenchantment.

"When they recruited us for missionary service, they told us amazing stories of God's workings. They said nothing about the sickness, loneliness, discouragement, conflicts, financial struggles, and the sending of our children off to college. Missionary life is nothing like they said it would be. It's living in the trenches."

Many missions agencies, recruiters and resources seek to cast vision and enthusiasm into new candidates heading off to the field. Rightly so, but often those same souls pumped full of optimistic reassurance, head to their fields unprepared for the vast challenges awaiting them.

Maybe this is one of the principal reasons missionary attrition rates are so high in the first few years of service?

Also, few aids exist to help weary and worn torn missionaries returning to their home countries with wounds they often will never overcome. As they reenter life at 'home' they fade into the fabric of their passport-culture slipping into anonymity.

Paul—the first missionary of the church—suffered harsh persecutions, deprivations and sufferings. Missionaries today should expect such travails.

When Missionaries Quit

Several sources state the average length of missionary service is twelve years.[78, 79] Data on the length of missionary service is dated. It extrapolates the percentages and numbers from missionaries who served decades ago.

My read is that the average time spent on the field, not in training fundraising, furloughs, and home assignments, is well under four years of service. With modern travel, many missionaries spend as much or more time at 'home' than in the field.

A couple in their middle 30s felt called to a country in South America. They trained, went through the approval process of a missions agency, and raised their support. Leaving for the field fully funded, and with over $40,000 dollars for setup costs, supporters felt betrayed when the couple resigned after only three months.

When pressed for a reason as to quitting after so short a time, they responded, "It just wasn't what we thought it'd be."

The Hard Truth

The missionary calling is a call to struggle in realms that affect our being's mental, emotional, and spiritual centers. Paul reminded us of this in his letter to the church in Ephesus:

Be strong in the Lord and in his mighty power. Put on all of God's armor so that you will be able to stand firm against all strategies of the devil.

167

For we are not fighting against flesh-and-blood enemies, but against evil rulers and authorities of the unseen world, against mighty powers in this dark world, and against evil spirits in the heavenly places.

Ephesians 6:10-12

This struggle Paul describes makes me think of the battles between good and evil in the comic book *Marvel Universe Series* produced by Walt Disney Studios through Marvel Studios LLC. Here's what I took away from those amazing stories connected by the theme of overcoming evil throughout 23 movies in the series.

The battle from beginning to end was not so much in the incredible action scenes of its characters like Iron Man, Thor, Black Panther, and the rest; it was rather in the plot behind those characters. A narrative that did not appear completely until the ultimate battle in *Avengers: Endgame*, when the Marvel superheroes defeated the evil Thanos.

It was in the ultimate battle that Thanos' depth of evil revealed itself. The hardships and suffering of every superhero found purpose and meaning when Thanos turned to ashes. As the superheroes triumphed, it was only then that the powers of darkness revealed themselves.

We sort of figure the characters in the Bible are like those superheroes in the comic books. People of such extreme faith that they sailed through all their voyages, unaffected by the trauma of it all. Well, you can write a movie script in that fashion, but it's not how life plays out, even for a missionary.

Our spiritual battles are dangerous. Count on the upcoming clashes. Prepare for them. Endure them like a dutiful soldier of Jesus Christ. 2 Timothy 2:3

Vicarious Trauma

Cross-cultural workers witness myriads of traumatic injuries and deprivations. The American Counseling Association notes:

> It is believed that counselors working with trauma survivors experience vicarious trauma because of the work they do. Vicarious trauma is the emotional residue of exposure that counselors have from working with people as they are hearing their trauma stories and become witnesses to the pain, fear, and terror that trauma survivors have endured. [80]

Other terms for vicarious trauma are secondary trauma stress, secondary victimization, and compassion fatigue. For me, *compassion fatigue* accurately describes my downward mental health spiral in the last years of serving in South Africa. Seeing hundreds of Zulu children die took its toll upon me. Added to that was a moderate brain injury I suffered.

Unknowingly, I became detached, numb, and uninterested in the very people I served. In caring, I ceased to care. Not because of lack of desire, but because caring overwhelmed my already spent soul and mind.

The Missionary's Mental Health

When speakers herald a message from air-conditioned buildings to patrons sitting in cushioned chairs of, "Just Trust God," I often think, "True, but just wait until..."

Some successful missionaries find themselves on stages, talking of their breakthroughs and achievements. But rarely do we invite a missionary to share their loneliness, depression, anxiety, or anger.

We protect ourselves behind masks of success and spirituality, fearing supporters might cease financing our endeavors if they knew our genuine struggles. One missionary revealed, "If they knew how screwed up I really am, they'd drop me in a heartbeat."

We frequently talk with missionaries who struggle with anxiety, depression, compulsive disorders, suicidal ideology, and secret struggles. As one missionary revealed, "I've never told anyone this ever before."

There's no shame in recognizing and admitting you've got a problem. The shame is perhaps in not getting help for your problem.

It's a rugged battle out there on the field. Mental faculties strain to cope with the stress and pressures of missionary life. For some, those pressures overwhelm the brain's coping mechanism to deal with trauma situations, like me, who suffers from PTSD.

PTSD is a trauma-induced affliction upon the brain resulting from an extreme single traumatic event or a series of traumatic occurrences. It happens when the brain's coping mechanisms become overwhelmed, rendering the brain unable to cope with trauma forced upon an individual.

Recently, a group of PTSD veterans invited me to join their group, which meets twice a month. Not being a Veteran of military service, the invitation both surprised and honored me. All suffered from Post-Traumatic Stress Disorder.

While sharing my PTSD struggles with those veterans, I concluded:

"I know my PTSD is not the same as yours."

Then one veteran interrupted.

"Don, you've experienced some of the same stuff we did just without a gun in your hands."

The similarities between my new found veteran friends and missionaries are intriguing. One sizeable difference is that veterans' options to receive help far outweigh what's available for missionaries.

Financial resources for missionaries to receive diagnosis, treatment, recovery, and healing are limited by their support levels.

Too many times—way too many—missionaries crossing our paths cry, "Once I came off the field and left missionary service, they forgot about me." Somehow we have to do better here.

170

Just yesterday, a missionary arrived here at Shepherd's Missionary House here in Grandbury, Texas. As Kathy and I listened to her story, she revealed an added fear.

"I've fought my feelings about all of this, and finally, I saw a Christian therapist. Some of my friends told me I lacked faith, especially since I'm taking medication to help me deal with it."

Another missionary witnessed the necklacing of four men in South Africa. Necklacing is the horrible murder of people by binding them inside a car tire and setting it alight. The victim burns to death. That missionary was me.

You never forget the smell of burning flesh. Or the smell of gangrene-infested-rotting flesh. Or the stench of a dead, decaying body.

What am I trying to say? Mental health is difficult to understand. I wish a simple prayer of faith could always heal mental illness. It doesn't. Faith in God to help me walk through my mental illness is more where I'm at these days. By his stripes, we are healed. Isaiah 53

The Missionary's Spiritual Health

Spiritual disciples—our alone-time with God—must take priority. Only in Christ do we suffer well while finding purpose and reason to endure.

I have found that spiritual health closely aligns with spiritual discipline. Many Christians are unfit because they are undisciplined. [81]

Busyness, the needs of the ministry, and demands of people dampen regular connections with Christ, the Scriptures, and prayer. Drifting away from the Captain of our souls, we float into dangerous waters of apathy and spiritual despondency.

When mental or spiritual health is chaotic, often both deteriorate. Here are some spiritual disciplines to consider:

171

1. *Prayer* – Don't worry about anything; instead, pray about everything. Tell God what you need and thank him for all he has done. Philippians 4:6

2. *Study*. Learn to enjoy God as you study your Bible. Reading my Bible, I often ask myself, "God, where are you on these pages. How can I know you better? Enjoy you more. Understand your ways."

3. *Fasting*. Fasting is a focused time of spiritual dependence upon God. To accomplish this, we abstain from food. By learning to deprive ourselves of self-indulgences, we can focus upon God to grow in our mutual relationship.

4. *Worship*. Worship points us to God's worthship; how much we value God in our actions and thoughts. Finding time to respond to God's worthiness redirects us towards God.

   Give to the LORD the glory he deserves! Bring your offering and come into his presence. Worship the LORD in all his holy splendor.

   I Chronicles 16:29

5. *Fellowship*. Where do you get your encouragement? I'm often amazed at how many missionaries while busying themselves in their work for God, spending most of their energies serving others, develop few—if any—deep, meaningful friendships.

   We need each other. Together, the embers of a fire glow red-hot, but scattered, they soon grow cold. Apart from each other, we grow cold too. The discipline of fellowship is important.[82]

6. *Celebration*. Missionaries often wade into intense human suffering. I know firsthand how other's tragedies can dampen the soul. Find time

to celebrate. Find things to observe. Enjoy the people in your life. Cast your gaze away from tragedy from time to time and take in the immense beauty of this planet. Give your soul a break. Breathe in fresh air.

For me, during my years in South Africa, celebration occurred twice a year with a group of Christians from the Emmaus Walk Movement in the mountains of Natal, South Africa. Spending an entire week with other Christians focusing upon God's gifts in our lives rejuvenated my soul.

Learn to rejoice in the little things too. Our favorite place of rejoicing was Wimpy's coffee shop in Ladysmith, South Africa. A cup of Wimpy's coffee gave me reason to celebrate. I love coffee.

Celebrate your victories. Your children. Each and any friend God puts in your path. Celebration keeps abated the gloomy clouds of discouragement and joylessness so prevalent in many missionaries today.[83]

For Kathy and me, this last chapter of our lives is a voyage of missionary caring for battered and bruised missionaries returning home in disbelief at the suffering which berated them in their ministries.

Developing a theology of suffering based upon the Scriptures prepares for the inevitable; that suffering is part of Christian service.

At some point, we will experience the end of pain and a ceasing of tears as God restores our bodies to immortal vitality. But that time is not this now. It has yet to reveal itself.

A proper theology of suffering enables cross-cultural workers to endure the hardships of missionary life. Dwelling upon suffering takes our eyes off the prize. That prize is Jesus Christ, for he is our example. By his stripes we are healed, and we must move forward even if that means we minister—like Jacob—with a limp. Genesis 32:31-32

 Sail On

In suffering, we can see Jesus. For it is in suffering that we identify most with him.

 True North

As the Scriptures say, "For your sake we are killed every day; we are being slaughtered like sheep."

Romans 8:36

For the more we suffer for Christ, the more God will shower us with his comfort through Christ.

2 Corinthians 1:5

Instead, be very glad—for these trials make you partners with Christ in his suffering, so that you will have the wonderful joy of seeing his glory when it is revealed to all the world.

1 Peter 4:13

Light House

Keep a lookout for the rocks of suffering that lie beneath your calling to service. Learn to sail, navigating around them rather than dashing yourself upon them. And, in your darkest hours, remember that *the Lord is your fortress; your God is the mighty rock where you hide.* Psalm 94:22

The joy of the Lord is our strength. So too, our smile.

Survival Tip #13

Lament – Express Your Emotions to God

On the tenth day of the tenth month in the ninth year of his rule, King Nebuchadnezzar of Babylon and all his army came against Jerusalem.

2 Kings 25:1

A LAMENT CARRIES THE IDEA of immense grief and sorrow. The word contains the notion of a chant, dirge, to wail, or even singing to express a person's grief.

One-third of the Psalms express such life's heartaches and woes.

The book of Lamentations was written by the prophet Jeremiah.[84] It expresses an array of emotions. Jeremiah laments the sins of the people of Judah, debauchery and demise of King Jehoiakim, the destruction of Jerusalem,

176

and the personal losses Jeremiah himself suffered at the hands of the Babylonians.

Jehoiakim was arguably the worst of all of Judah's kings. Rabbinic literature declares him as a "Godless tyrant who committed atrocities and crimes. He lived in incestuous relations with his mother, daughter-in-law, and stepmother, and was in the habit of murdering men, whose wives he then violated and whose property he seized."[85]

Jeremiah castigated King Jehoiakim for his evil actions and prophesied the end of his reign:

> Why is this man Jehoiachin like a discarded, broken jar? Why are he and his children to be exiled to a foreign land? O earth, earth, earth! Listen to this message from the Lord! This is what the Lord says: 'Let the record show that this man Jehoiachin was childless. He is a failure, for none of his children will succeed him on the throne of David to rule over Judah.'

> Jeremiah 22:28-30

When King Jehoiakim heard of Jeremiah's writings, he ordered him before the royal court. After reading only four verses from one of Jeremiah's scrolls, he burned them. Jeremiah 36:21-25

In 587-586 B.C., King Nebuchadnezzar of Babylon destroyed the city of Jerusalem after a long siege. The devastation and destruction of the temple brought massive suffering upon the people of Judah.

The Book of Lamentations shrieks at the horrendous treatment of its people by the Babylonians:

> You have invited terrors from all around, as though you were calling them to a day of feasting. In the day of the Lord's anger, no one has escaped or survived. The enemy has killed all the children whom I carried and raised.

> Lamentations 2:22

177

THE NEBUCHADNEZZAR'S of this world often come up against those who dare enter the enemy's territory, sharing the Gospel of Jesus Christ. When encouraging people to trust solely in Jesus Christ who died in our place, pardoning us once and for all from our sins, the enemy will always respond.

I call this "Our Babylons." We should prepare and expect Babylon to meet us on our fields of service. And the Nebuchadnezzars of missionary work present powerful foes.

Some will object to the analogy claiming, "But hold on. Jerusalem was destroyed because of the sins of Judah." Are we not entering the Judahs of this world filled with people marred by sin's effects?

Remember that not every person was guilty in Judah during those days. The land held many innocents who suffered because of the sins of others.

Take the prophet Daniel, who, as a young child was removed from his family and enslaved. King Jehoiakim handed him over, along with his friends Hananiah, Mishael, and Azariah—otherwise known as Shadrach, Meshach, and Abednego—in the first deportation of Judah's citizens to Babylon.

> We should prepare and expect Babylon to meet us on our fields of service.

The prophet Jeremiah, while identifying with the misdeeds of Judah's people, serves faithfully, yet still suffers staggering losses. It's what we do with our losses that defines our lives and service.

Jesus told us that God gives sunlight and rain to both evil and good people. Matthew 5:45 Good people—innocent people—suffer from the bad of others.

Often, we cannot grasp mighty forces that come up against us as we attempt to proclaim Jesus Christ. The Nebuchadnezzars surrounding us will not leave us untouched, and we will suffer losses.

I've witnessed hosts of missionaries experience the most grievous of losses at the hands of the enemy. Horror stories exist beyond belief sometimes.

Just because we're missionaries doesn't mean God exempts us from the wounds of open spiritual warfare, the casualties that ensue. There are too many to count.

It's in our grieving and anguish that we can sense God's goodness. Jeremiah expresses this in his greatest anguish:

> The faithful love of the Lord never ends! His mercies never cease. Great is his faithfulness; his mercies begin afresh each corning. I say to myself, "The Lord is my inheritance; therefore, I will hope in him!"

> Lamentations 3:22-24

In our cozy sermons in the West, we often embrace these three verses as an assurance of a fuzzy feel-good accompaniment of God's enablement of good things on our behalf.

During my years in Africa, bereft Zulu Christians embraced God in their pain. They often screamed and cried, throwing themselves upon the ground in the angst of losing family members or experiencing a tragic loss. In their loss and grief, I often heard another verse from Lamentations quoted:

> The Lord is good to those who depend on him, to those who search for him.

> Lamentations 3:25

> To whom you lament is to whom you give yourself.

In lamenting, we either find or lose God. It's where we pull closer to God or lean away from him, drawing on our own emotional capacities. *To whom you lament in your deepest despairs is to whom you give yourself.* Learn to bring the Nebuchadnezzars of your life to God. Lament towards God rather than self, for self leads no further than itself.

179

Why Lamenting is Important

Again, fellow missionary care workers with whom we discuss such issues, cite missionaries need to bring their anguishes to God.

One shared, "Too many times I've watched a missionary shrivel up and become embittered with their outcomes of life. Rather than bring their misfortunes to God, they seek every other pathway to express their grief, never going to the only One who can sustain them."

If we don't turn to God with our betrayals, failures, losses, and grief, what happens with all our emotions? We then tend to:

Bemoan in anger.
Harbor bitterness.
Become self-righteous.
Judge others to harshly.
Carry a load of resentment towards God and people.
Turn to vices to help us forget our pain.
Blow up relationships with those who love us.
Lash out at anyone of a differing opinion.
Find fault with other's expressions of grief.

Don't agree? Well, hey, my friend. I was there, and I've watched many sink in the same waters. It's a resentful agnosticism that sets in when struggling to answer the question, "God, why me?"

Lamenting to God—expressing our deepest emotions—is necessary for a healthy life. It doesn't mean we forget. Or ever get over the loss of a spouse or child. It means we look beyond Babylon's devastation in our lives for God to heal our hurts.

We still hurt, but we hurt better. If that makes any sense. It's sort of how I understand it, anyway.

180

What's the alternative? We fight a hundred wars in our souls and minds over how things might have gone differently, who was to blame, and who we might exact revenge from.

The African people often amazed me at how they could get on with life in their personal injuries. Not one Zulu family out of a hundred in my congregations were spared a murder. Most families lost children before reaching their teenage years. All families experienced violence. And very few married couples reached their senior years without the loss of their spouses.

How did they handle life? Christians lamented, pouring out their emotions before God and people. After a period of grief, they got back to living.

That's one reason I don't care for the concept of celebrating at a funeral. Now, I'm not finding fault here, but within a fifteen-year span, Kathy and I lost ten family members. Several deaths occurred on Thanksgiving and Christmas. Yep, right smack on those very days. Death is untimely.

Now, you can celebrate life during deaths, but I find grieving is far more healthy for me. It's a personal experience not a criticism.

I can't celebrate my grandchild dying—SIDS—but I can grieve in hope. The hope that I will see Myra again. I get choked up just typing this sentence.

I can't celebrate Kathy's brother dying, but I can grieve in hope. I can't celebrate losing my dad, his brother, and sister within less than three years of each other, but I can lament in hope because God is bigger than all of that.

Mom and Harry—her husband—died within three weeks of each other. I didn't celebrate. I grieved.

Learning to Lament

In the West, we tend to think of the Psalms as a liturgy or sermon. It was, and is often the case today, that people sang many Psalms in their worship.

There are five kinds of psalms: praise, wisdom, royal, thanksgiving, and lament.[86]

To lament is a crying—or maybe yelling—prayer for help coming from pain, distress, betrayal, or disillusionment. Lamenting is quite common in the Bible. Over one-third of the psalms are laments.[87]

Sometimes lamenting Psalms are referred to as The Cursing Psalms. I like that. There have been times... well, let's leave that alone for now. But it does sort of reinforce some of my conversations with my God over the years.

Christina Fox, in her book, *A Heart Set Free: A Journey to Hope through the Psalms of Lament,* makes some brilliant observations regarding lamenting:

Dictionaries define the word lament as "feeling or expressing sorrow or grief." It's not a word we use much these days. In fact, lamenting is an art that we don't often practice in Western culture.

Rather than express our emotions, we tend to hide them, distract ourselves from feeling them, or even pretend they don't exist. When difficult circumstances cut into our lives, we are likely to seek out false saviors to rescue us.

We bury ourselves in work, entertainment, or a pint of ice cream. We might even take things into our own hands and attempt to control our circumstances. We'll do anything but face the pain and heartache we feel.[88]

How does lamenting apply to us practically? What about a circumstance that plowed you under, to use a Northern Minnesota farming term?

You know, that person or thing that tore your soul to where you ceased to catch the Holy Spirit's momentum and direction. When the words of the Bible seemed empty, and prayer felt meaningless.

Tragedies from the past that keep you awake at night and have you rehearsing scenarios repeatedly in your head a year later.

The reason you give when you say, "We used to, but because of _____ we don't anymore."

The hurt you carry with you every day.

The rejection you feel.

The trauma that changed who you are.

Those faces you still see.

The constant transitions of missionary life.

That which controls you.

The feeling that somehow God's abandoned you.

The disappointment you can't shake.

Look at Psalms 13 for a model of lamenting:

Turn towards God rather than self. David looked to God with the "Why's" of his situation:

> *O Lord, how long will you forget me? Forever?*
> *How long will you look the other way?*

Bring your complaints and objections to God. Most laments in the Bible contain grumbling and protests aimed at God because of predicaments of life. David complains:

> *How long must I struggle with anguish in my soul,*
> *with sorrow in my heart every day?*
> *How long will my enemy have the upper hand?*

Demand God's help. David made bold requests to God:

> *Turn and answer me, O Lord my God! Restore the sparkle to my eyes, or I*
> *will die. Don't let my enemies gloat, saying,*
> *'We have defeated him!'*
> *Don't let them rejoice at my downfall.*

Then, Choose to trust God with your losses.

But I trust in your unfailing love. I will rejoice because you have rescued me. I will sing to the Lord because he is good to me.

Lamenting is a prayer language for Christians who live in a sin-stained, marred world. To cry is human; to lament is reaching toward the divine.[89]

Jesus himself lamented to his Father in the Garden of Gethsemane. He cried, "Abba, Father, everything is possible for you. Please take this cup of suffering away from me." Mark 14:36

On the cross, Jesus cried out in agony, repeating the words of Psalm 22, "My God, my God, why have you forsaken me…?"[90]

Let God Become Your Burden-Bearer

Lamenting is a turning to God when sorrow tempts you to run from him.[91] While commanded to carry one another's burdens, the Bible is also replete with crying and complaining to God. Not in the sense of ingratitude, but rather in a spirit of, "GOD HELP ME!"

Unless you learn to unload all of that stuff onto the broad everlasting shoulders of the Father, you will wither in the emotional conflicts warring inside your soul. Bottling up your missionary stress, complexities, and challenges can rip your soul's sails, leaving you drifting aimlessly, turning you into a disillusioned deckhand.

YOU WILL suffer betrayal, fail a time or two or three, and you will most likely fall ill. An illness you'll carry the rest of your life if you spend much time on the field. Some supporters will abandon you. Missionaries will turn on you. Someone may rip away the work that you labored diligently to establish over the many years.

How will you handle all of this? How will you express your heartaches and emotions? Your anger? Your frustrations? Your faith imperfections? Will you bury them deep inside to eat away at you until there is nothing left? Or lash out at others, blaming them for your misfortunes?

The most soulful healthy answer is, "Tell it to God. Lament your woes to your Creator."

When You're Disappointed

When you're disappointed with God's interactions in your life, instead of recycling your perceived misfortunes repeatedly in your mind until you're a cranial zombie, try expressing your inmost turmoil to God:

O Lord, how long will you forget me? Forever?
How long will you look the other way?
How long must I struggle with anguish in my soul,
with sorrow in my heart every day?
How long will my enemy have the upper hand?
Turn and answer me, O Lord my God!
Restore the sparkle to my eyes, or I will die.
Don't let my enemies gloat, saying, "We have defeated him!"
Don't let them rejoice at my downfall.

Psalms 13:1-4

Or, how about these words from the sons of Korah, written to lead the people of Israel in worship:

Wake up, O Lord! Why do you sleep?
Get up! Do not reject us forever.
Why do you look the other way?
Why do you ignore our suffering and oppression?
We collapse in the dust,
lying face down in the dirt.

Rise up! Help us!
Ransom us because of your unfailing love.

Psalm 44:23-26

You say, "Oh, I couldn't say that to God!" I used to feel that way, but I've learned that God wants to hear our desperate cries of the soul.

When You're Angry

Asaph is one of my heroes in the Bible. He asked the same questions I've asked:

Pour out your wrath on the nations that refuse to acknowledge you—
on kingdoms that do not call upon your name.
Why should pagan nations be allowed to scoff,
asking, "Where is their God?"
Show us your vengeance against the nations,
for they have spilled the blood of your servants.
O Lord, pay back our neighbors seven times
for the scorn they have hurled at you.
Then we your people, the sheep of your pasture,
will thank you forever and ever,
praising your greatness from generation to generation.

Psalm 79:6,10, 12-13

Whew, brutal honesty with God. Respectful talk, but angry. Authentic, the kind God accepts, hears, and to which he responds. God wants to hear such expressions.

If we don't go to God with such emotions, how will those emotions find release? In our health, attitudes, and relationships, that's how.

When Depressed and Feeling Alone

The ancient songwriter lamented:

> Turn to me and have mercy,
>   for I am alone and in deep distress.
> My problems go from bad to worse.
>   Oh, save me from them all!
> Feel my pain and see my trouble.
>   Forgive all my sins.
> See how many enemies I have
>   and how viciously they hate me!
> Protect me! Rescue my life from them!
>   Do not let me be disgraced, for in you I take refuge.

Psalm 25:16-20

Those kinds of words often find their expression on Facebook posts and social medias in not so eloquent of words. Rather than bare our souls in a fit of rage or sarcasm on social media, why not take them to God?

God designed us to express our emotions and lamentations to him.

Learning to Trust God

> Many people say, "Who will show us better times?"
>   Let your face smile on us, Lord.
> You have given me greater joy
>   than those who have abundant harvests of grain and
>   new wine.
> In peace I will lie down and sleep,
>   for you alone, O Lord, will keep me safe.

Psalms 4:6-8

Biblical lamenting—sharing your soul's deepest sentiments—can mark the difference between sailing the high seas of missionary service or floundering adrift.

There's an old German Hymn translated into English called *Tell it to Jesus Alone*. I love the words of that old song.

Are you weary, are you heavy hearted?
Tell it to Jesus, tell it to Jesus.
Are you weary, are you heavy hearted?
Tell it to Jesus, tell it to Jesus.
Are you grieving over joys departed?
Tell it to Jesus alone.

Are you weary, are you heavy hearted?
Tell it to Jesus, tell it to Jesus.

Are you grieving over joys departed?
Tell it to Jesus alone.

Tell it to Jesus, tell it to Jesus,
He is a Friend that's well known.

You've no other such a friend or brother,
Tell it to Jesus alone.

Do the tears flow down your cheeks unbidden?
Tell it to Jesus, tell it to Jesus.

Have you sins that to men's eyes are hidden?
Tell it to Jesus alone.
Tell it to Jesus, tell it to Jesus,
He is a Friend that's well known.

You've no other such a friend or brother,
Tell it to Jesus alone.

188

Do you fear the gathering clouds of sorrow?
Tell it to Jesus, tell it to Jesus.

Are you anxious what shall be tomorrow?
Tell it to Jesus alone.

Sail On

That darkest moment in your life; a betrayal, death, loss of a friend, or opportunity. Something that was taken from you that can never be replaced. That event in your life that hounds you. What's that moment? Describe that niggly throbbing inside that you struggle to let go.

_____

_____

_____

_____

_____

_____

Where or to whom do you ever express your pain? Your anger? The sense of loss? A stolen innocence?

Lamenting—a moaning, crying out, complaining, or regret—offers a release, a letting of painful emotions flow.[92] Refusing to release angst allows pressure to build, eventually rupturing some part of your life. Open the pressure valve of lament. It's healthy for both body and soul.

189

Rolling our mental anguishes unto God allows disengagement from any anxiety that controls the mind. Sharing with other wayfarers enlists a team to help carry one's burdens.

Lament. Cry out. Give your emotions to God. Declare your faults and failures to dependable others. *A burdened shared is often a burden carried.*

 True North

O Lord, God of my salvation, I cry out to you by day. I come to you at night. Now hear my prayer; listen to my cry. For my life is full of troubles...

Psalm 88:1-3

The Lord is close to the brokenhearted; he rescues those whose spirits are crushed.

Psalm 34:18

 Light House

When peace like a river, attendeth my way,
When sorrows like sea billows roll
Whatever my lot, thou hast taught me to say
It is well, it is well, with my soul.

It Is Well With My Soul
by Horatio Spafford

Survival Tip #14

Make Prayer Your

Highest Priority

Prayer blows God's presence and
peace upon us during the most tempestuous times of life

My entrance into the world of prayer began in January 1973, when on a cold winter's night, I crawled out of bed and kneeled, putting my faith in Jesus Christ. Since then, God and I converse often.

People sometimes ask, "But how do you know God is really real?" My answer is always the same.

I know God is real because he answers my prayers. God ALWAYS answers my prayers. All the time.

Not that my prayers are nobler than any other missionary, but when I pray, God responds. God answers not because of the greatness of my prayers but because of the vastness of his person and promises. "How much more will your heavenly Father give good gifts to those who ask him."–Jesus Matthew 7:11

Now, I wouldn't say that I'm a great *pray-er*, but I will declare that God is a great answerer. Wow, has he answered my prayers over the years, and… often beyond my expectations.

My father, after I led him to Christ, often commented, "Bud, It seems like every time you need something God is right there for you."

God is always there for me. God is there for you. Our Emmanuel, Jesus, ensures this. God being right there for us, and we being right there with him; this is the essence of prayer.

I think probably the most important element of prayer is not as much in the answers to our prayers, but the oneness we experience with God in praying. That a being who painted the universe with a finger of immense power allows us—specks upon a planet which is but a speck among trillions of other planets, in a galaxy that's a mere speck among 200 billion other galaxies—to interact with Him whenever we want.

As I read about people of the past who prayed like E. M. Bounds, Andrew Murray, J. I. Packer, Evelyn Christenson, Martin Luther, Timothy Keller, Madame Jeanne Guyon, D. L. Moody, Rosalind Goforth, or R. A. Torrey, their passion for prayer consumes me at times.

A friend recently put me onto *The Kneeling Christian by Unknown Author*. In the book, the unknown writer talks of meeting a missionary who shared many wonderful things God was doing through his ministry. When asked as to the reason for such success, the missionary replied, "*I find it necessary, oftentimes, to spend four hours a day in prayer.*" Wow!

This writer sums up well the challenge many of us experience with prayer:

How few there are among us who know what prevailing prayer really is! Every one of us would confess that we believe in prayer, yet how many of us truly believe in the power of prayer?

A missionary friend of mine—Gail Gritts—who has served for years in England put it this way:

> Prayer is one of the most disregarded ministries among missionaries and pastors....but I have found...it is the work of the ministry...nothing happens of any eternal value without it, and when we partner with God through prayer there is no limit to what He can do!

What really bakes my noodle about all of this is that I'm unable to comprehend the incalculability of God's willingness to allow us—*me*—to interact freely with the Creator at any time of my choosing. Think of it.

Now, I've never prayed four hours straight, but in my attempts to talk with God, my prayer life has developed into three practices. I think of them as the 3 C's of my prayer life.

Now, while this sounds sophisticated, it's not. It's nothing more than practical personal attempts at prayer in my life.

My 3 C's are to pray *contemplatively, conversationally,* and *collaboratively with God.*

Contemplative Prayer

Contemplative prayer is often credited as a Catholic practice and sometimes linked to centering prayer; a meditative practice of self-awareness.

I'm referring to my personal prayer practice, attempting to contemplate God's incalculable greatness, and his willingness to interact with me. Like a friend who spends time with another friend enjoying and valuing relationship.

It's prayer that contemplates—muses, gazes, or ponders—God. I often ponder God.

My contemplative praying tries to clear out other considerations and clutter from my mind and fixate upon the Maker of this universe, God's vastness, accessibility, and majestic being. Meditating and thinking about my Abba—Father.

Or, to focus upon God as King David did:

When I look at the night sky and see the work of your fingers—
the moon and the stars you set in place—
what are mere mortals that you should think about them,
    human beings that you should care for them?

Psalms 8:3-4

Nature is probably one of my best places to contemplate God. During my days in South Africa, I often took my dogs up the rocky terrain behind my house and sat on a large rock waiting for sunrise. As the sun came up, I'd comment, "God, you do outstanding work."

Last night here in Texas, I looked up towards the West just after sunset to view the coming Great Conjunction of 2020. This event marks when Jupiter and Saturn will appear closer to each other since the 13th century.

The two celestial bodies shine steadily, unlike the twinkling stars in the sky. In a few days, they will appear to join, forming a single elongated brightness in the coming together of the two planets.

The media are referring to this event as the Christmas Star. It is a once and a lifetime event which last occurred on March 4, 1226. Johannes Kepler in the 17th century speculated that the star that led the Wise Men from the East to Bethlehem for the birth of Jesus was such a conjuncture.[93]

God, you do outstanding work.

Sometimes, early in the darkness of my room, I'll just lay in my bed, focusing upon God in complete stillness. It takes practice to clear your mind, to pay attention only to God. Knowing that God is near, right there, Emmanuel; God with us.

Imagine, the God who is above all, in all, and over all, being present with just little old me. Now, that's something to contemplate.

Sometimes, I will pray selected Psalms out loud, seeking to focus upon God as did those ancient songwriters of worship.

Contemplative praying also keeps The Greatest Commandment in view. It makes sure that my prayers don't become more about me than God.

It's important to pray for myself and others, but those needs must not center my prayer thoughts above God. God is the object of prayer, not myself or others. We often let prayer become more about us than God.

In keeping with the Shema in Deuteronomy 6:5, "And you must love the Lord your God with all your heart, all your soul, and all your strength," Jesus taught us to pray. The Lord's Prayer—as we call it—modeled for us by Jesus focuses the first half of the prayer upon God alone.

> Our *Father* who art in Heaven,
> Hallowed be *thine name*,
> *Thine Kingdom* come,
> *Thy will* be done,
> On earth as it is in Heaven...

Contemplative prayer then is above all, time set aside to focus entirely upon God. Making sure that God is in every part of my life.

Conversational Prayer

The only way I've figured out how to pray without ceasing—as Jesus instructed us to do—is by conversational prayer. Conversational prayer is simply that, having conversations with God. Conversing with God like he's actually there. Because... he is!

Sitting next to you in the car.
Working out with you at the gym.
Walking through the isles at the grocery store with you.
Sitting in the dentist's chair when they start drilling. Ouch.
With you during your lowest of lows.

The celebrations.

Your beginnings.

The closures of life.

Losses.

Gains.

And the joyous of joys.

When I remember to focus on God, my mind, and sometimes my tongue, chats with the Almighty even in the most routine of activities.

Hey Father, help that woman there who's struggling.

God, provide for the needs of that poor child.

God, assist the EMS crew working on that wreck on the Southbound side of the road. Help them help those who are injured.

God, forgive me for that thought.

For those words.

For my response.

For my anger.

Help missionary M_____ who's in ICU with Covid right now.

God, help my grandchild A_____ with her learning disability. Give mom and dad patience and wisdom.

Help my son with his new job.

Bless those pastors in that special meeting today.

Hey God, how's it going today?

How are you doing?

Thanks for being you.

Conversational prayer is brief short expressions to God. It focuses on worship of the Savior, intercession for others, confession of sin, and thankfulness to God.[94]

With hands-free cellular devices, drivers passing from the opposite direction assume I'm talking on the phone when I'm actually often talking with God.

Try it. Learn to be in the habit of conversation, talking with God every day, all day long.

When you take that sip of Starbucks coffee driving off in your car, "Ah, God this is good. Isn't it?"

When uncertain, "God what are you doing now?"

When that driver cuts you off on the road.

In any activity, talk with God.

When is the last time that you actually talked with your Creator in everyday conversational words? We talk with those we value. How much then do we value God?

Collaborative Prayer

A "collaboration" is "Produced or conducted by two or more parties working together."[95]

Praying collaboratively is a coming together with God about an issue or direction in my life. Not taking a step until I'm confident that God is leading in a particular way.

There are three facets of this third part of my praying; collaborating with God, others, and self.

Collaborating with God

Collaborating with God leads me into real interactions with God. Two Scriptures set the fulcrum for such exchanges:

Take delight in the Lord, and he will give you your heart's desires.

Psalms 37:4

197

Trust in the Lord with all your heart; do not depend on your own understanding. Seek his will in all you do, and he will show you which path to take.

Proverbs 3:5-6

Ever asked yourself the question, "Why isn't prayer a higher priority in my life?" I've found the answer to that question is:

*When I don't enjoy prayer it's because
I'm not enjoying God,
When I'm enjoying prayer it's because
I'm enjoying God.*

When do we enjoy God? When we're in frequent collaboration with Abba about our lives, relationships, and ministries.

Let me give you a personal example:

In the 90s, in South Africa, sensing a need to build a facility to help train caregivers caring for myriads of orphans in the area, I began seeking God's guidance. Climbing that same rocky path behind my home, often in the morning's coolness, I looked over an empty field across the street from our home.

Many times I asked God to give me the property to build a facility. When a white developer purchased all the adjacent land, including that empty field, I scheduled an appointment with him.

Sitting down in his office, I got right to the point.

"Leonard, I hear you are going to build a huge housing development across from my house. A nice church and children's facility would help attract many families."

He looked at me and spouted, "Mingo, what do you want?"

I replied, "I want that empty field by the Mkhamba trees."

"Not on your life," he responded.

With a handshake, I left his office.

The following week he called me back to his office.

"Don, I don't know why I'm doing this, but I'll give you that property to build a church and children's facility."

Smiling, I added, "I've been collaborating with God on that property for a long time, asking him if he might give it to me."

Leonard laughed.

Then I immediately followed with another request.

"Hey, Leonard, ah… you know that building next to the empty property."

"Yes, what about it, Don?"

Cautiously I almost whispered, "Well, can I have that too?"

He erupted, "Mingo! Get out!"

But you know what? He gave me the building as well. That was all fine and good, but that was all I had—A piece of land and an old building needing a makeover.

The next month, a gentleman called me and asked to meet. He mentioned Leonard spoke with him and offered to pay for his services, helping me develop an architectural plan for a suitable facility.

Standing on the property and sharing my thoughts, he drew splendid drawings of the future facility and handed them to me the next week.

Then we figure the price of such a facility.

How about $300,000?

Well, I didn't possess that kind of money, so we boarded a plane and headed back to the States with a sense of God's direction in the venture.

At the very first church, we presented our vision—I mean the very first church—a couple approached us. We met, and after several discussions, they offered to finance the whole project. THE WHOLE THING!

Today sits a glorious facility in Mkhamba Gardens, Ladysmith, South Africa, where hundreds of care providers are trained, and they assist multitudes of women and orphans.

God, you do amazing work.

Now, I'd like to tell you that this resulted from a process of painstaking prayer. But God simply provided that which we often discussed together on a cliff behind my house. God's Spirit shaped my dreams of such a place and brought people alongside us to accomplish the building of the facility.

Collaborating with Others

The early church knew what it meant to collaborate in prayer. Acts 2:42 & 6:4.

After the ascension, 120 people gathered together to pray for eight days. Acts 1:14 tells us, "They all met together and were constantly united in prayer…"

After the release of Peter and John from prison, they gathered together with other believers and prayed. Acts 4:23-31

When James was murdered, and Peter imprisoned, what did the church do? They gathered for prayer and talked with God about the situation. Acts 12:5

When Peter's chains fall off, releasing him from prison, he went to a house where "many were gathered in prayer." Acts 12:12

Leaders of the church in Antioch prayed and worship. As they collaborated in prayer, the Spirit called Paul and Barnabas for missionary service. Acts 13:3

During Paul's journey he met the elders of the Ephesus church on a beach praying. Acts 20:36

I'd like to have been present at those prayer get-togethers. Where people skipped meals, set aside time, met together, and conversed with God. Often I ask myself, "I wonder what those prayers were like?"

Was it taking 30 minutes of requests and closing with a quick individual prayer?
Or individuals praying after each other one at a time?
A few praying for all?

Everyone talking to God out loud simultaneously?

Moments of silent contemplation?

How did they center themselves upon God?

How much prayer did they focus on themselves? How much on others?

It was an honor to know Dr. Kenneth Connolly. He was born in Sutherland, England in 1927, and pastored several churches before coming to the United States under the auspicious of the Billy Graham Association in 1966.

Teaching at Baptist Bible College in Springfield, Missouri, and Pacific Coast Baptist Bible College in California, he often spoke as a guest speaker worldwide, lecturing extensively on the life of Christ and the Reformation.[96]

It was my pleasure to know him the last twenty-five years of his life. He often spoke about the Welsh Revival in Wales, England 1904-05.

His Grandfather—Peter Connolly—took part in the Welsh Revival and shared his many experiences with his grandson Kenneth. One particular conversation still resonates with me.

Ken began in his Scottish brogue, "My grandfather described one of the revival meetings."

After praying all day, we went out to the coal mines—in Scotland—and prayed again. From the mines emerged blacken figures of men covered in a day's work of coal dust. Only the eyes of men peering through flickering candle lanterns revealed that men stood before us. The blackness of the coal dust otherwise blended those men into the night's darkness.

We shared God's message of forgiveness of sins, and salvation through his son Jesus Christ. As the night went on, tears of these hardened men washed small lines of coal dust away from their faces.

All the men's faces showed lines of pale white skin where coal dust covered them before the meeting began. The entire crew turned to Jesus that night.

When asked about the essentials of such a revival, Dr. Connolly replied in his Scottish brogue—can hear my grandfather it like it was yesterday— "Prayer. Without prayer, there is no revival."

The Great Awakening in the 1740s was tied to people praying together.

In the 1850s, The Great Prayer Revival that exploded across the United States with thousands gathering to pray together started with six men praying together.

In the 1860s, Charles Spurgeon's church in London had prayer meetings every morning and every evening.[97]

In 1984, a group of Anglo Christians erected a tent in the village of Matiwane, nestled in the mountains of Northern Natal, South Africa. Holding evangelistic gatherings for ten days, two young Zulu men put their faith in Jesus Christ during that tent meeting. The event changed their lives.

Weeks later, Cyrial and Mandla met with a small group of teenage Zulu Christians. Having just discovered Christ, they searched for a church to attend that taught the Bible. They were unsuccessful.

Deciding to meet on their own, they wondered how to begin. So, every Friday on a mountain ridge overlooking Matiwane, a small group of Zulu teenagers met and prayed that God might send someone to help them.

In 1986, we arrived in Ladysmith, South Africa. Our first Sunday in the country we visited a Zulu church. That morning a youth ensemble sang. At one point Cyrial asked the congregation to pray that God might send someone to help them with their fledgling church.

The next Sunday, we stood before that group of Zulu teens sharing our story of God's leading us to Matiwane. It marked the first organized service for the new church. Cyrial and Mandla hailed the meeting as a result of two years of prayer. The collaborative prayer of a group of Zulu teenagers launched our ministry.

Collaborating by Myself

This is my prayer closet of private prayer. It is a simple approach I use to shape prayer times with God.

Find a place.
Make a time.
Do it.
Be consistent.

Find a place to pray. Sometimes it is in the darkness of my lounge with noise cancelling-headphones on that I meet with God. Other times it was in the Great Smokey Mountain. The Drakensberg Mountains of South Africa was also a favorite place. These days it's often on the porch looking at Lake Granbury.

Carve out a time to pray. I'm an early morning person, so effective prayer comes best in the early hours. It's the time when my mind is alert and focused.

Regular interaction with God is the aim.

Then longer prayer periods are needed. Setting aside a day, or a week, for interaction with God. Prayer walks, prayer retreats, journeys, and trips.

Finding a place for extended times with God is—well, for me—magic. A refocus and refreshing found in prayer..

And then do it. Be intentional. Set your times with God as the highest of priorities.

It's the ask, seek, and knock that Jesus talked about in Matthew 7:7-12.

A few examples stick out in my life.

In 2014, we resigned the church I pastored to begin a ministry of caring for missionaries. Kathy and I moved in with our oldest son's family.

For nine months I was unemployed. This gave me a long extended season of meeting with God every morning.

That was the most refreshing time of my life. During that time, my journaling took off—journaling that resulted in writing three books.

In 2015, we started living like missionaries again—two homeless old people moving from one place to another, trying to raise support for a new out-of-the-box missionary ministry. Some superb churches allowed us to stay in their missionary houses and apartments during this time.

One Monday morning in our third year of transitional living, I received a phone call. A woman named Cora shared that her friend saw our presentation the evening before at church, piquing her interest to contact me.

She asked, "Could we get together and meet for lunch?"

The next week Kathy and I sat with Gary and Cora, discussing our hearts for our new missionary ministry. As a Vietnam Vet, Gary understood PTSD and showed much interest.

During the meal, right out of the blue, they proposed that we come and live on their property on the lake. There we could conduct our ministry.

I was very apprehensive about the idea. In the past, people often offered such kindnesses. Then, unintentionally, they expected responses or favors from us in return that we could not give.

Such letdowns resulted in disappointment with us or a sense of betrayal. Well-meaning people felt unappreciated because we couldn't respond in a way they desired.

Three weeks later, Cora called me again. We set up a second meeting at a local restaurant in Granbury, Texas. During the meal, Gary asked me the reason for my hesitation.

I responded, "Gary, I don't want to hurt or disappoint you when we can't fulfill an expectation you might have for us."

Gary looked me in the eye and said, "Don, we only want to invest in your ministry. There is no quid pro quo here." Being a lawyer, Gary spoke his language to me.

The next day, we walked to the property next to theirs on Lake Granbury, Texas. Cora pointed out the wreck of a small home they intended on buying and remodeling. Cora asked, "Can we call it Shepherd's House." I smiled.

With the three cottages they owned next to the property, missionaries who needed our help could stay during their visit.

Upon our agreement, they drained all their financial liquidity in the venture. In August 2018, we moved into the Shepherd's House. Rent free, it relieved us from a tremendous amount of monthly support we would otherwise have needed to raise.

To date, over 100 missionaries have stayed with us.

Yet, we struggled to raise finances for our basic needs. Raising support for missionary living and ministry is tough on the best of days.

I don't think we'll ever raise—in the traditional sense—the financial support other missionaries acquire to finance their ministries. What we do is not glamourous like other missionary ministries.

But you know what? God reminds us that he is not limited in providing for our needs. God supplies in unique ways.

A doctor attended one of our presentations. Afterwards, he approached, mentioning that he wanted to invest in our ministry. So now, that GP doesn't charge us for his services.

How much monthly financial support is that worth?

Hang on; there's more.

I desperately needed dental care. During a mission conference I spoke at two years ago, a professionally dressed woman approached me in the lobby after the Sunday morning service.

She explained that she was a dentist and owned her own practice. She offered, "If you need a checkup, I'd love to invest in your ministry by offering to look at your teeth. No charge." What?

During our nine years of pastoring in Minnesota, we couldn't afford dental care. So, the morning we entered her office, it was the first time seeing a dentist in over ten years.

Kathy came out with flying colors. No cavities. No problems. I however, received a different diagnosis. After over two hours of dental x-rays, and then more x-rays, and still a third round of x-rays, the dentist asked to meet with me.

"Ok, Don, here's the story. The three crowns you currently have need replacing. You need at least two root canals and crowns to go with them, and you have 13 cavities."

Whaaaaaaaaaaaaaaaaaaaaaaaaaaaaaat?

Over the past two years, that wonderful dentist and her team of professionals took care of all my dental needs along with follow-up visits too. The cost? Nothing.

Now, how much monthly support is that worth?

Missionary, God has more than one way to meet your financial needs. He owns it all and disperses it according to his good pleasure. All we need do is seek, ask, and knock at the door of prayer.

Excel in Prayer

The lack of prayer is the Achilles heel of many cross-cultural workers. We're too busy. We forget. One day blends into another without a sense of God's presence in our lives because we unintentionally close God off from our activities by our prayerlessness.

> The lack of prayer is the Achilles heel of many cross-cultural workers.

When we do finally pray, we center much praying upon ourselves; our desires for more or less, and our wants for friends and family.

We need to examine our prayer habits. Many resources exist to help us improve in praying. Here are a few:

- *Life's Limitless Reach* by Jack Taylor.
- *Prayer: Experiencing Awe and Intimacy with God* by Timothy Keller
- *E.M. Bounds on Prayer*

- *Fervent: A Woman's Battle Plan to Serious, Specific, and Strategic Prayer* by Priscilla Shirer
- *Psalms: The Prayer Book of the Bible* by Dietrich Bonhoeffer
- *Praying with the Psalms: A Year of Daily Prayers and Reflections on the Words of David* by Eugene H. Peterson
- *Andrew Murray: Collected Works on Prayer: 7 Books in 1* by Andrew Murray
- *The Ministry of Intercession (Updated and Annotated): A Plea for More Prayer (Murray Updated Classics Book 1)* by Andrew Murray
- *The Battle Plan for Prayer: From Basic Training to Targeted Strategies* by Stephen Kendrick and Alex Kendrick
- *The 28-Day Prayer Journey: A Daily Guide to Conversations with God* by Chrystal Evans Hurst

Jesus taught that people *should always pray*. Luke 18:1 Our best example of praying is Jesus. Matthew 6:9-13

Our Father, which art in heaven—Focus on God

Hallowed be thy name—Center on God's Holiness

Thy Kingdom come—Acknowledge God's Dominion

Thy will be done on earth—Seek God's Intentions

As it is in heaven—Gain Heaven's Perspective

Give us this day our daily bread—

Ask for daily Needs

And forgive us our trespasses—Confess Sin

As we forgive them that trespass against us—

Forgive Others

And lead us not into temptation—

Rely upon God

But deliver us from evil—

Seek God's Guidance

For thine is the kingdom—

Accept God's Ownership

The **power**— Submit to God's Control

and the glory—Recognize God's Incredibleness

For ever and ever—Perceive the Way it will Be

Amen—Make it so

Never Give Up!

Therefore, since we are surrounded by such a huge crowd of
witnesses to the life of faith,
let us strip off every weight that slows us down,
especially the sin that so easily trips us up.
And let us run with endurance the race
God has set before us.

We do this by keeping our eyes on Jesus,
the champion who initiates and perfects our faith. Because of the
joy awaiting him, he endured the cross, disregarding its shame.
Now he is seated in the place of honor
beside God's throne.

Think of all the hostility he endured from sinful people; then you
won't become weary and give up.
After all, you have not yet
given your lives in your struggle against sin.

Hebrews 12:1-4

And, please remember to smile.

Other books by Don Mingo

All books listed are available through Amazon, Kindle, other book distributors, or through donmingobooks@gmail.com

The Faith Principle – 4 Secrets to Making Your Faith Work Again.

So, You Want to Be A Missionary: Essential Considerations.

Son Risings – Discovering and Caring for the Real You.

To Hell, Back and Beyond: A PTSD Journey – When Faith and Trauma Collide.

Life Boundaries – Balancing Career, Marriage, Relationships, and the Important Stuff of Life.

Boundaries – 5 Steps to Getting Your Life Back.
Helping people overcome pornography addiction through transformation of the mind. Available at donmingobooks@gmail.com

Get Your Life Back! Journal. A 21-week addiction renewal journal.

For special rates contact at donmingobooks@gmail.com

1 https://bethanygu.edu/missions/missionary-etymology/
2 Joel Whitburn's Top Pop Singles 1955-1990 – ISBN 0-89820-089-X
3 https://en.wikipedia.org/wiki/SS_Edmund_Fitzgerald
4 Queen of the Lakes. Detroit: Wayne State University
Press. (1994). ISBN 0-8143-2393-6.
5 Thompson, Mark L. (1991). *Steamboats & Sailors of the Great Lakes*. Detroit:
Wayne State University Press. ISBN 0-8143-2359-6. Retrieved November 18,2012.
6https://en.wikipedia.org/wiki/SS_Edmund_Fitzgerald#cite_note-
FOOTNOTEThompson1994164-5
7 https://www.mlive.com/news/2017/11/8_facts_behind_the_edmund_fitz.html
8 https://en.wikipedia.org/wiki/SS_Edmund_Fitzgerald
9 https://www.collinsdictionary.com/us/dictionary/english/normal
10 https://www.lexico.com/en/definition/normal
11 http://www.dictionary.cambridge.org/us/dictionary/english/expectation
12 http://www.macmillandictionary.com/us/dictionary/american/expectation
13 Ibid.
14 http://www.dictionary.com/browse/expectancy?s=t
15 https://en.wikipedia.org/wiki/SS_Daphne_(1883)
16 Reed, Edward James (1883). Report On The "Daphne" Disaster. London: Eyre and
Spottiswoode. Retrieved 2009-08-15
17 https://en.wikipedia.org/wiki/SS_Daphne_(1883) #cite_note-3
18 https://www.sciencedaily.com/terms/anchoring.htm
19 Public domain. Westbrook, Francis B. (1903-1975) © Oxford University Press, London
20https://www.baptistpress.com/resource-library/news/imb-1132-missionaries-staff-
accept-vri-hro/
21http://www.christianitydaily.com/articles/5704/20150827/southern-baptist-
convention-go-up-800-missionaries-personnel.htm
22 https://en.wikipedia.org/wiki/Epictetus
23 Young, Sarah (2004). *Jesus Calling*: Thomas Nelson,146.
24 Psalms 46:1 KJV
25 https://www.catholic.com/tract/sign-of-the-cross
26 1 Corinthians 10:31
27 John Bunyan, Grace Abounding to the Chief of Sinners," p. 173, Emerald House, 1998
28 *Giants of the Missionary Trail* (1954). Scripture Press Foundation, 73.
29 https://believersweb.org/view.cfm?ID=43
30 https://www.desiringgod.org/messages/how-few-there-are-who-die-so-hard
31 https://www.preceptaustin.org/adoniram_judson
32 https://www.desiringgod.org/messages/how-few-there-are-who-die-so-hard

[33](Adoniram Judson, "Advice to Missionary Candidates," Maulmain, June 25, 1832, as quoted by https://www.desiringgod.org/messages/how-few-there-are-who-die-so-hard

[34] Ibid.

[35]https://www.imb.org/2018/11/27/missionaries-you-should-know-lottie-moon/

[36] Catherine B. Allen, The New Lottie Moon Story (Nashville: Broadman Press, 1980

[37] *Biographical Dictionary of Christian Missions,* Macmillan Reference USA, copyright © 1998 Gerald H. Anderson, New York, NY.

[38]https://www.imb.org/lottie-moon/givelottie-moonpromotional-materialswho-was-lottie-moon/lottie-quotes/

[39] https://www.speedandsmarts.com/toolbox/articles2/smallboat-sailing/getting-the-most-from-your-sails

[40] James 1:15

[41] http://www.joethorn.net/blog/2014/9/7/personal-holiness

[42] http://www.biblestudytools.com/commentaries/robertsons-word-pictures/mark/mark-8-32.html

[43] https://en.wikipedia.org/wiki/D._T._Niles

[44] David J. Bosch, A Spirituality of the Road, page 70, 1979 ISBN 1-57910-795-8.

[45] Curt Thompson, Anatomy of the Soul, page 53, 2010 ISBN 978-1-4143-3415-8.

[46] Anthony J. Paone, My Daily Bread, p. 341-343, TAN Books, 2015 ISBN 978-1-61890-812-4.

[47] Ibid.

[48] https://scottattebery.com/christian-living/weve-already-died/

[49] https://madmissions.com/2018/12/our-friend-john-chau-a-buried-seed/

[50]https://www.mayoclinic.org/diseases-conditions/agoraphobia/symptoms-causes/syc-20355987

[51] Walter Scott, The Lay of the Last Minstrel 1805

[52] https://www.merriam-webster.com/dictionary/attrition

[53] https://en.wikipedia.org/wiki/Cultural_relativism

[54] https://www.robertwelch.com/customer/pages/how-to-set-a-table

[55] https://www.robertwelch.com/customer/pages/how-to-set-a-table

[56] https://www.alifeoverseas.com/traveling-missionaries/

[57] Ibid.

[58] https://en.wikipedia.org/wiki/Florence_Nightingale

[59] https://www.christianitytoday.com/ct/2013/may/how-missionaries-are-changing-medicine.html

[60] Ibid.

[61] Ibid.

[62] https://www.christianitytoday.com/news/2017/january/outstanding-medical-missionary-burundi-gerson-lchaim-prize.html

[63] Mingo, Don. So You Want to Be a Missionary: Essential Considerations. Mingo Coaching Group, 2019. Page 43.

[64]https://www.marineinsight.com/guidelines/dry-dock-types-of-dry-docks-requirements-for-dry-dock/

[65] https://www.gotquestions.org/Lord-of-the-Sabbath.html

[66] https://www.who.int/mental_health/evidence/burn-out/en/

[67] https://en.wikipedia.org/wiki/Holmes_and_Rahe_stress_scale

[68] https://www.stress.org/holmes-rahe-stress-inventory

[69]   https://blogs.ethnos360.org/brian-pruett/2012/03/23/just-how-stressed-are-missionaries-and-what-can-we-do-about-it/

[70]Stewardship of Self for Christian Workers: Stress. Ron Koteskey & Marty Seitz http://www.missionarycare.com/pdfs/ChristianWorkers-Stress.pdf

[71] Ibid.

[72] http://www.jewishencyclopedia.com/articles/8235-isaiah

[73] https://safeplaceministry.org/

[74]https://www.psychologytoday.com/us/blog/the-power-rest/201705/rest-success

[75] Ibid.

[76]
https://www.blueletterbible.org/lang/lexicon/lexicon.cfm?Strongs=G1377&t=KJV

[77] http://www.tribune.org/a-remarkable-life/

[78]
https://www.worldevangelicals.org/resources/rfiles/res3_95_link_1292358708.pdf

[79]   https://www.alifeoverseas.com/what-is-the-average-length-of-service-for-missionaries-on-the-field-the-long-and-the-short-of-it/

[80]   https://www.counseling.org/docs/trauma-disaster/fact-sheet-9---vicarious-trauma.pdf

81 Brandon Hilgemann. 12 Spiritual Disciplines That Will Make Your Faith Strong. May 9th, 2018. https://www.propreacher.com/12-spiritual-disciplines-that-will-make-your-faith-strong/

[82] Ibid.

[83] Ibid.

[84] 2 Chronicles 35:25

[85] https://en.wikipedia.org/wiki/Jehoiakim

[86]https://www.enotes.com/homework-help/there-5-kind-psalms-praise-wisdom-royal-392689

[87]https://www.franciscanmedia.org/biblical-laments-prayer-out-of-pain/

[88]https://www.ligonier.org/blog/way-lament/

[89] Ibid.

[90] https://www.franciscanmedia.org/biblical-laments-prayer-out-of-pain/

[91] https://www.desiringgod.org/articles/dare-to-hope-in-god

[92]https://www.psychologytoday.com/us/blog/spiritual-wisdom-secular-times/201609/lamentation-can-be-good-thing

[93] https://www.npr.org/2020/12/09/944560103/jupiter-and-saturn-will-be-together-again-for-the-holidays

[94]   https://www.cru.org/us/en/train-and-grow/help-others-grow/mentoring/conversational-prayer-revives.html

[95] https://languages.oup.com/google-dictionary-en/
[96] http://www.kenconnolly.org/biography.htm
[97] https://eph5v2.wordpress.com/2011/06/15/praying-together-examples/

Made in the USA
Middletown, DE
20 April 2021